OAE Middle Grades Math (030) Exam #1

Test Taking Tips

☐ Take a deep breath and relax

☐ Read directions carefully

☐ Read the questions thoroughly

☐ Make sure you understand what is being asked

☐ Go over all of the choices before you answer

☐ Paraphrase the question

☐ Eliminate the options you know are wrong

☐ Check your work

☐ Think positively and do your best

Table of Contents

TEST DIRECTION

DIRECTIONS

Read the questions carefully and then choose the ONE best answer to each question.

Be sure to allocate your time carefully so you are able to complete the entire test within the testing session. You may go back and review your answers at any time.

You may use any available space in your test booklet for scratch work.

Questions in this booklet are not actual test questions but they are the samples for commonly asked questions.

This test aims to cover all topics which may appear on the actual test. However some topics may not be covered.

Studying this booklet will be preparing you for the actual test. It will not guarantee improving your test score but it will help you pass your exam on the first attempt.

Some useful tips for answering multiple choice questions;

- Start with the questions that you can easily answer.

- Underline the keywords in the question.

- Be sure to read all the choices given.

- Watch for keywords such as NOT, always, only, all, never, completely.

- Do not forget to answer every question.

1

A satellite travels 1,420,000,000 km in its orbit around the sun in 1,8 years. Which of the following is closest to the average speed of the satellite, in meter per second, in its orbit around the sun?

A) 12,508

B) 25,016

C) 45,028

D) 600,372

2

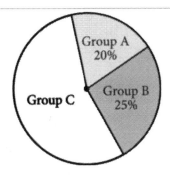

The distribution of student groups in a trip is given above.

If 165 students are from Group C, how many students are from Group A?

A) 60

B) 75

C) 80

D) 100

3

$$\frac{4}{0.01} + \frac{0.4}{0.04}$$

What is the equivalent of the expression above?

A) 110

B) 114

C) 401

D) 410

4

	Rock	Pop	Total
Ages 16-17	22	73	95
Ages 17-18	41	44	85
Total	63	117	180

A survey was conducted in the United Kingdom regarding music preferences. Given on the table above is the data of 180 randomly selected teenagers aged 16 to 18.

According to these data, which of the following is the percent that represents those who listen to pop music?

A) 20%

B) 35%

C) 50%

D) 65%

5

$$\sqrt{4} - \sqrt[3]{-8} + \sqrt{(-2)^4} \div \sqrt[4]{(-4)^2}$$

What is the result of the operation given above?

A) 2

B) 3

C) 4

D) 6

6

Costs Comparison of Toys		
Toys	Cost at Fred's Toys	Cost at Ann's Toys
Shopkin	$25	$24
Minion	$40	$46
Barbie	$35	$30

If a customer receives a 25% discount from Fred's Toys and a 35% discount from Ann's Toys, how much more would he pay, in dollars, to buy a minion and a shopkin from Fred's Toys than Ann's Toys?

A) $3

B) $3.25

C) $4

D) $4.75

7

If $a - b = 0$ then which of the following should be equivalent to $a + b$?

A) a^2

B) 0

C) $\dfrac{a}{b}$

D) $2b$

8

Price of Socks in Store A	
Brown	$ 2 per 5 batches
Black	$ 3 per 7 batches
Blue	$ 5 per 9 batches
Orange	$ 7 per 11 batches

Which color of socks cost the most per batch in Store A?

A) Brown

B) Blue

C) Black

D) Orange

CONTINUE ▶

9

Anthony studied a lot and increased his SAT test score from 1,200 to 1,500. What is the percent increase of his score?

A) 20

B) 25

C) 30

D) 40

10

$$\frac{\sqrt{n}}{4} = 3\sqrt{2}$$

What is the value of n in the equation given above?

A) 24

B) 72

C) 288

D) 576

11

Isotopes	Percent Abundance
24 amu	78.70%
25 amu	10.13%
26 amu	11.17%

Average atomic mass and percent abundances of three isotopes of Magnesium are given in the table above. What is the average mass of magnesium, in amu?

A) 24.3

B) 24.8

C) 25.2

D) 25.6

12

$$\frac{1}{\dfrac{1}{x+1} + \dfrac{1}{x+2}}$$

Which of the following is equivalent to the expression above?

A) $\dfrac{x^2 + 3x + 2}{2x + 3}$

B) $2x + 3$

C) $x^2 + 3x + 2$

D) $\dfrac{2x + 3}{x^2 + 3x + 2}$

13

Type K trees produce 20% more apples than Type L trees.

Based on this observation, if the Type K trees produced 156 apples, how many apples did the Type L trees produce?

A) 120

B) 130

C) 144

D) 168

14

$$(2^{-2}+2^{0})\cdot 5$$

What is the result of the operation given above?

A) 0.25

B) 1.25

C) 6.25

D) 20

15

$$5^{x+2}=\left(\left(\left(\frac{1}{7}\right)^{3}\right)^{0}\right)^{41}$$

What is the value of x that satisfies the equation given above?

A) -3

B) -2

C) -1

D) 1

16

Dominant Color	Large	Small	Total
Green	--	3	--
Blue	6	--	--
Total	--	--	25

Ricardo classified his favorite paintings hanging in an art gallery by both size and dominant color. The results are in the table above. Ricardo found that 40% of his favorite paintings were green.

How many of Ricardo's favorite paintings are small and have blue as the dominant color?

A) 4

B) 6

C) 9

D) 15

17

The square of a positive number is the same as 5 times the number added by 36. What is the square root of that number?

A) 3

B) 4

C) 9

D) 16

18

$$\sqrt[3]{9^{x-2}} = 81$$

What is the value of x in the equation given above?

A) 1

B) 2

C) 4

D) 8

19

If $\dfrac{a}{b} = \dfrac{2}{3}$, what is the value of $\dfrac{a+b}{a-b}$?

A) -5

B) -3

C) -1

D) 5

20

Which of the following lists of numbers is arranged in ASCENDING order?

A) 5913, 5914, 5967, 5975, 5963, 5970, 5976

B) 5808, 5823, 5863, 5886, 5943, 5929, 5924

C) 5813, 5846, 5897, 5901, 5939, 5945, 5996

D) 5808, 5853, 5831, 5907, 5917, 5915, 5927

21

Hamburger (Per Day)				
Student year	0	1	2 or more	Total
Freshman	15	11	11	37
Sophomore	6	22	28	56
Junior	8	9	51	68
Senior	1	4	34	39
Total	30	46	124	200

A survey was conducted among a random sample of students in a high school cafeteria about hamburger consumption. The results per daily consumption are given in the table above.

Which of the following statements is supported by the data given in the table?

A) A higher percentage of seniors than sophomores eat one hamburger.

B) A higher percentage of juniors than freshman eat two or more hamburgers.

C) 60% of all students surveyed eat the hamburger.

D) 6% of sophomores do not eat the hamburger.

22

3 scruples = 1dram
3 drams = 1ounce
12 ounces = 1pound

Based on the information given in the table above, if you use 45 scruples of a medicine per day for 12 days, this will be how much total medicine in pounds?

A) 5

B) 12

C) 60

D) 75

23

$$\frac{m}{n} = 3 \qquad 15\frac{n}{m} = A$$

What is the value of A?

A) 5

B) 18

C) 45

D) 60

24

$$\sqrt{0.09} - \sqrt{0.16} + \sqrt{0.49}$$

What is the result of the operation given above?

A) 0.2

B) 0.4

C) 0.6

D) 0.8

25

People are standing in a line to get on the bus. As Edison stood in the line, he noticed that there are 9 more people behind him than there is in front of him. If the total number of people in the line is 3 times the number of people in front of him, then how many of the people in the line are behind Edison?

A) 9

B) 10

C) 19

D) 30

26

$$
\begin{array}{r}
75 \\
24\overline{)1{,}804} \\
\underline{168} \\
124 \\
\underline{120} \\
4
\end{array}
$$

Manuella turned on her computer, checked in for her flight and left home to go to the airport. She forgot to turn off the computer while she was leaving home and the computer was on for 24 hours a day for 1,804 hours. Manuella did the work above to determine how many days the computer was on.

Manuella needs to finish the calculation to find how long, in days, the computer was on. Which statement about Manuella's calculations is true?

A) Manuella can complete the calculation by adding on 0.4 of a day since the remainder is 4 and found that the computer was on for 75.4 days.

B) Manuella can complete the calculation by dividing 24 ÷ 4 to get 6 and found that the computer was on for 75.6 days

C) Manuella can complete the calculation by dividing 4 ÷ 24 to get 0.16 and found that the computer was on for 75.16 days.

D) Manuella can complete the calculation by subtracting 24 − 4 to get 20 and found that the computer was on for 75.20 days.

27

A baseball team won a games and lost b games. What part of its games did it loss?

A) $\dfrac{a}{a+b}$

B) $\dfrac{b}{a+b}$

C) $\dfrac{a+b}{a}$

D) $\dfrac{a-b}{a}$

28

$$\frac{2x}{x+3} \div \frac{12}{3x+9}$$

Which of the following is equivalent to the expression above given that $x \neq -3$?

A) $\dfrac{x}{2}$

B) $2x$

C) $3x$

D) $8x$

29

The Environmental Protection Agency (EPA) identifies contaminants to regulate in drinking water. According to the drinking water regulations of EPA, the maximum amount of nitrate that can be present in water is 15 milligrams per liter. A scientist is measuring the amount of nitrate in a local lake to see if it is safe to drink. The scientist takes a sample of 25 liters of water. If the number of milligrams per liter of nitrate in the lake water is 40% of the maximum value that is safe to drink, how many grams of nitrate should the scientist expect to find in her sample?

A) 0.15 g

B) 0.375 g

C) 6 g

D) 15 g

30

$$2x = y = 7z$$
$$2x + y + 7z = 42$$

What is the value of $x + y + z$?

A) 20

B) 21

C) 22

D) 23

31

$$\frac{a}{b} = \frac{c}{d}$$

Based on the equality above, which of the following expression is true?

A) $\dfrac{a-b}{b} = \dfrac{c+d}{d}$

B) $\dfrac{a-d}{b} = \dfrac{c-b}{a}$

C) $\dfrac{a+c}{c} = \dfrac{c+d}{b}$

D) $\dfrac{c+d}{c} = \dfrac{a+b}{a}$

32

$$\sqrt{\frac{1}{9}+\frac{1}{16}}$$

What is the result of the operation given above?

A) 0.143

B) 0.286

C) 0.417

D) 0.583

33

If buying n pizzas cost p dollars, then how much will it cost to buy m pizzas at the same rate?

A) $\dfrac{pm}{n}$

B) $\dfrac{m}{pn}$

C) mpn

D) $\dfrac{mn}{p}$

34

I. $\dfrac{a}{a+b}$ II. $\dfrac{b}{a+b}$ III. $\dfrac{a+b}{a}$ IV. $\dfrac{a-b}{a}$

A baseball team won a games and lost b games. What part of its games did it lose?

A) I

B) II

C) III

D) IV

35

If $\dfrac{x-1}{3}=k$ and $k=3$, what is the value of x?

A) 2

B) 4

C) 9

D) 10

36

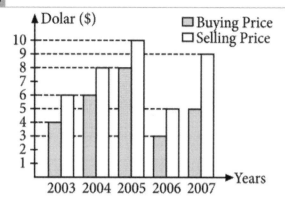

The column chart given above shows the buying and selling prices of items sold in a store between 2003 and 2007.

How many percents is the profit margin of the store in 2007?

A) 40

B) 50

C) 80

D) 90

37

Four years ago, Nathaniel bought a car for $9,300 which is now worth $5,700.

What is the percentage of depreciation of his car?

A) 38%

B) 38.7%

C) 59.3%

D) 63.15%

38

A lemonade mixture calls for a 75% pure water and 25% lemon extract. How many glasses of water must be added to a 4 glasses of lemon extract to make the lemonade mixture?

A) 7.5

B) 8

C) 12

D) 20

39

A	K	O	R	Z
1	2	3	4	5

Which of the following choices contains the letters add up to 9 after they are converted to numbers?

A) K, R, Z

B) O, A, R

C) O, R, Z

D) A, O, Z

40

In a book store books cost $18 each and notebooks cost $10 each. Sera buys n books, b notebooks and pays D dollars Which of the following equation represents for the number of notebooks bought?

A) $\dfrac{D+18n}{10}$

B) $\dfrac{D-18n}{10}$

C) $\dfrac{18n-D}{10}$

D) $\dfrac{D-10n}{18}$

41

Stephanie does push-ups and sit-ups every morning. She does p push-ups and $2p+5$ sit-ups.

Which statement describes the number of sit-ups Stephanie does every morning?

A) The number of sit-ups is 5 more than half the number of push-ups she does.

B) The number of sit-ups is 5 fewer than half the number of push-ups she does.

C) The number of sit-ups is 5 more than twice the number of push-ups she does

D) The number of sit-ups is 5 fewer than twice the number of push-ups she does.

42

A fruit salad is made from bananas, pears and strawberries mixed in the ratio of 2 to 5 to 3 respectively by weight. What fraction of the mixture by weight is pears?

A) $\dfrac{1}{2}$

B) $\dfrac{2}{3}$

C) $\dfrac{3}{5}$

D) $\dfrac{3}{10}$

43

The length of one piece of pipe is 6 inches more than three times the length of a shorter section. If the length of the longer pipe is 33 inches, what is the length, in inches, of the shorter pipe?

A) 9

B) 10

C) 11

D) 13

44

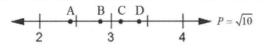

Use the number line given above to answer the following question.

Which point on the number line is the best approximation for P?

A) Point A

B) Point B

C) Point C

D) Point D

45

Age (years)	Male	Female	Total
0-20	54	70	124
21-40	94	86	180
41-65	114	142	256
65+	88	102	190
Total	350	400	750

The age and gender distribution of a random sample of people from a population is given in the table above. If the whole population consists of 12,000 people, which of the following statements is true?

A) It is expected that there are 6,400 males in the population.

B) It is expected that there will be 1,824 females between 41 and 65 years old in the population.

C) It is expected that there will be 1,376 females between 21 and 40 years old in the population.

D) The number of males in the population can not be estimated with the information given.

46

$$-1 < a < 0 < b < 1$$

Which of the following is NOT true?

A) $b^2 < b$

B) $a^2 > a$

C) $a^3 < a$

D) $b^3 > a^3$

47

If $2r = 3k$ and $5k = 7p$, then find p in terms of r?

A) $\dfrac{10}{21}r$

B) $\dfrac{21}{10}r$

C) $\dfrac{2}{7}r$

D) $\dfrac{2}{15}r$

48

In a class of 56 students 37 are taking Statistics, 29 are taking Calculus. Of the students taking Statistics or Calculus, 11 are taking both courses. How many students are NOT enrolled in either course?

A) 1

B) 11

C) 18

D) 44

49

If $2^{10} = a$, then what is the equivalent of $2^{10} + 2^{11}$ in terms of a?

A) $2a$

B) $3a$

C) $11a$

D) $21a$

50

$$5A = 3B \qquad \frac{4}{B} = \frac{C}{3} \qquad \frac{C}{D} = 5$$

Based on the relations given above, which of the following statements is not true?

A) A and B are directly proportional.

B) B and C are inversely proportional.

C) A and C are inversely proportional.

D) A and D are directly proportional.

51

Which comparison is true?

A) $8.5 < \sqrt{18} < 9.5$

B) $17 < \sqrt{18} < 19$

C) $4 < \sqrt{18} < 4.5$

D) $4.5 < \sqrt{18} < 5$

52

A is 25% of B and C is 10% of B. What percentage of C is A?

A) 15

B) 25

C) 35

D) 250

53

$$5x - 9 \geq 6x - 7$$

Which of the following numbers is not a solution of the inequality given above?

A) -1

B) -3

C) -4

D) -5

54

The expression $\dfrac{3x-4}{x+2}$ is equivalent to which of the following ?

A) $3-\dfrac{10}{x+2}$

B) $3+\dfrac{2}{x+2}$

C) $3+\dfrac{10}{x+2}$

D) $3-\dfrac{2}{x+2}$

55

If the school is 12 miles away from Anne's house and Starbucks is 4 miles away from the school, which of the following conclusions must be true?

A) Starbucks is exactly 8 miles from Anne's house.

B) Anne's house is closer to the school than Starbucks.

C) Anne's house is east of the school.

D) Anne's house is at most 16 miles from Starbucks.

56

A specific DNA sequencing machine can identify the sequence of base pairs of a DNA, taking approximately 10 seconds to sequence 1,000 base pairs.

If a researcher wants to sequence a gene made up of 150,000 base pairs, how many minutes would it take for him to get the sequences?

A) 25

B) 60

C) 150

D) 1,500

57

If $\dfrac{a+b}{a}=6$ then what is $\dfrac{a+b}{b}$?

A) $\dfrac{8}{7}$

B) $\dfrac{6}{5}$

C) $\dfrac{4}{3}$

D) $\dfrac{3}{2}$

CONTINUE ▶

58

If is $12 + 3x$ is 11 less than 36, what is the value of $12x$?

A) 52
B) 140
C) 148
D) 236

59

Michael leaves his house and bikes south at a constant speed of 8 miles per hour. His dad, John, leaves the same house three hours later, driving south at a constant speed of 12 miles per hour.

How long will it take for dad, John, in hours, to reach the son, Michael?

A) 2
B) 3
C) 4
D) 6

60

An office has two stapling machines. Machine K staples a batch of paper in 12 hours and Machine L staples same batch of paper in 3 hours. How long would it take to staple 5 batch of paper if two machines work together?

A) 2.4
B) 5
C) 12
D) 17

61

$$5^{-2} + 5^{-1} + 5 = N$$

What is the value of N given above?

A) -10
B) 25
C) 5.24
D) 0.24

62

A piece of cloth which is 75 cm long and 32 m wide can be produced with 15 kg of cotton.

How many meters wide of cloth that is 80 cm long can be produced with 12 kg of cotton?

A) 12
B) 24
C) 36
D) 96

63

On a map, 1 centimeter represents 8 kilometers. What area is represented by a square on the map with a perimeter of 24 centimeters?

A) 48 square kilometers
B) 192 square kilometers
C) 2,304 square kilometers
D) 36,864 square kilometers

64

In November, the price of GSM Controlled Automatic Cooking Machine was $150. In December the price increased by 12 percent. During a sale in January, the December price was discounted by 14 percent.

What was the price of the item during the sale in January?

A) $144.48

B) $148

C) $150.48

D) $162

65

$$\frac{1-\dfrac{1}{x}}{1+\dfrac{1}{x}} = 3$$

What is the value of x?

A) -3

B) -2

C) -1

D) 1

66

The price of 500 mg L-Ribose is $18. L-Ribose is cretaed with 90% purity. If a customer orders $90 of L-Ribose, it will contain what amount of pure L-Ribose?

A) 0.25g

B) 2.25g

C) 2.5g

D) 2.75g

67

$$a = \frac{7.2b^3}{c^2}$$

The relation between a, b and c is given above. What happens to a when both b and c are doubled?

A) Halved

B) Doubled

C) Quadrupled

D) Multiplied by 8

68

Mae fed $\dfrac{1}{11}$ of the ducks at a farm. Which decimal is equal to the fraction of ducks Mae fed?

A) $0.\overline{01}$

B) $0.0\overline{1}$

C) $0.\overline{09}$

D) $0.0\overline{9}$

69

Isabel has some coins in her pocket consisting of dimes, nickels, and pennies. She has three more nickels than dimes and two times as many pennies as nickels.

If the total value of the coins is 72 cents, how many nickels does she have?

A) 3

B) 4

C) 6

D) 8

71

Harris wants to divide number N by 6, but, by mistake, he pushes 8 button of the calculator instead of 6 and gets a result which is 10 less than the correct answer. Which of the following equations determine N ?

A) $\dfrac{N+10}{8}$

B) $\dfrac{N}{8} - \dfrac{N}{6} = 10$

C) $\dfrac{N}{8} + 10 = \dfrac{N}{6}$

D) $\dfrac{N}{6} + \dfrac{N}{8} = 10$

70

Alicia is a student at Ridgewood High School. She surveyed a random sample of the sophomore class of his high school to determine whether the Spring Festival should be held in April or May. Of the 80 students surveyed, 30% preferred April and the rest preferred May.

According to this information, about how many students in the entire 240 person class would be expected to prefer having the Spring Festival in May?

A) 56

B) 72

C) 96

D) 168

72

If the sum of two consecutive integers is 17, what is their product?

A) 30

B) 48

C) 56

D) 72

73

A rectangle was altered by changing its length and width. Its length is increased by 20 percent and its width is decreased by k percent. If these alterations increased the area of the rectangle by 8 percent, what is the value of k?

A) 8

B) 10

C) 15

D) 20

74

The price of an antique increased by 20% but is then decreased by 20%.

Which of the following is the overall change of the initial price?

A) No change

B) Reduced by 20%

C) Raised by 4%

D) Reduced by 4%

75

If $\dfrac{a}{3} = \dfrac{b}{5}$ then what is $\dfrac{ab + a^2}{a^2 + b^2}$?

A) $\dfrac{17}{20}$

B) $\dfrac{12}{17}$

C) $\dfrac{5}{34}$

D) $\dfrac{8}{34}$

76

When a ball bounces it reaches three-fourths of its previous height with each bounce.

How high was the ball when it was dropped if it reached a hight of 54 cm after the third bounce?

A) 72

B) 96

C) 128

D) 256

77

Two numbers differing by 4 has a sum of m. What is the value of the bigger number in terms of m?

A) $\dfrac{m-4}{2}$

B) $m-4$

C) $\dfrac{m-4}{2} + 4$

D) $\dfrac{m-4}{2} - 4$

78

$$m(x + 3) = 2x - m + 1$$

For which value of m does the equation above have no solution?

A) -4

B) -1

C) 2

D) 3

20

CONTINUE ▶

79

I. $\dfrac{AB}{12C}$ II. $12\dfrac{AC}{B}$ III. $\dfrac{12C}{AB}$ IV. $\dfrac{BC}{A}$

A dozen apples cost a total of B dollars. At this rate, which of the equations given above can be used to find the number of apples that can be bought for C dollars?

A) I

B) II

C) III

D) IV

80

If the sum of two integers is 20, which of the following cannot be their product?

A) –125

B) –21

C) 19

D) 80

SECTION 1 - ARITHMETIC

#	Answer	Topic	Subtopic	#	Answer	Topic	Subtopic	#	Answer	Topic	Subtopic	#	Answer	Topic	Subtopic
1	B	TSATMC	SSATMC1	21	B	TSATMC	SSATMC2	41	C	TSATMA	SSATMA3	61	C	TSATMB	SSATMB5
2	A	TSATMC	SSATMC2	22	A	TSATMC	SSATMC2	42	A	TSATMC	SSATMC1	62	B	TSATMC	SSATMC1
3	D	TSATMB	SSATMB7	23	A	TSATMC	SSATMC1	43	A	TSATMA	SSATMA3	63	C	TSATMC	SSATMC2
4	D	TSATMC	SSATMC2	24	C	TSATMB	SSATMB6	44	C	TSATMB	SSATMB12	64	A	TSATMC	SSATMC2
5	D	TSATMB	SSATMB6	25	C	TSATMA	SSATMA3	45	C	TSATMC	SSATMC2	65	B	TSATMB	SSATMB7
6	B	TSATMC	SSATMC2	26	C	TPRXSAB	SPRXSAB1	46	C	TSATMA	SSATMA1	66	B	TSATMC	SSATMC2
7	D	TSATMC	SSATMC1	27	B	TSATMC	SSATMC1	47	A	TSATMC	SSATMC1	67	B	TSATMC	SSATMC1
8	D	TSATMC	SSATMC1	28	A	TSATMB	SSATMB7	48	A	TSATMA	SSATMA3	68	C	TSATMB	SSATMB7
9	B	TSATMC	SSATMC2	29	A	TSATMC	SSATMC2	49	B	TSATMB	SSATMB5	69	C	TSATMA	SSATMA3
10	C	TSATMB	SSATMB6	30	D	TSATMC	SSATMC1	50	D	TSATMC	SSATMC1	70	D	TSATMC	SSATMC2
11	A	TSATMC	SSATMC2	31	D	TSATMC	SSATMC1	51	C	TSATMB	SSATMB12	71	C	TSATMA	SSATMA3
12	A	TSATMB	SSATMB7	32	C	TSATMB	SSATMB6	52	D	TSATMC	SSATMC2	72	D	TSATMA	SSATMA3
13	B	TSATMC	SSATMC2	33	A	TSATMA	SSATMA1	53	A	TSATMA	SSATMA1	73	B	TSATMC	SSATMC2
14	C	TSATMB	SSATMB5	34	B	TSATMC	SSATMC1	54	A	TSATMB	SSATMB7	74	D	TSATMC	SSATMC2
15	B	TSATMB	SSATMB5	35	D	TSATMA	SSATMA1	55	D	TSATMC	SSATMC8	75	B	TSATMC	SSATMC1
16	C	TSATMC	SSATMC1	36	C	TSATMC	SSATMC2	56	A	TSATMC	SSATMC1	76	C	TSATMA	SSATMA3
17	A	TSATMA	SSATMA3	37	B	TSATMC	SSATMC2	57	B	TSATMC	SSATMC1	77	C	TSATMA	SSATMA1
18	D	TSATMB	SSATMB6	38	C	TSATMC	SSATMC2	58	A	TSATMA	SSATMA1	78	C	TSATMA	SSATMA1
19	A	TSATMC	SSATMC1	39	D	TSATMC	SSATMC4	59	D	TSATMC	SSATMC1	79	B	TSATMA	SSATMA1
20	C	TSATMB	SSATMB12	40	B	TSATMA	SSATMA3	60	C	TSATMA	SSATMA3	80	D	TSATMA	SSATMA1

Topics & Subtopics

Code	Description	Code	Description
SPRXSAB	Science	SSATMB6	Radicals & Radical Equations
SPRXSAB1	Mathematics	SSATMB7	Operations with Rational Expressions
SSATMA	Heart of Algebra	SSATMC	Problem Solving and Data Analysis
SSATMA1	Solving Linear Equations & Inequalities	SSATMC1	Ratios, Rates & Proportions
SSATMA3	Linear Equations & Inequalities Word Problems	SSATMC2	Percents & Unit Conversions
SSATMB	Passport to Advanced Mathematics	SSATMC4	Table Data & Probability
SSATMB12	Structure in Expressions	SSATMC8	Statistics & Data Inferences
SSATMB5	Exponents & Rational Exponents		

CONTINUE ▶

1

A satellite travels 1,420,000,000 km in its orbit around the sun in 1,8 years. Which of the following is closest to the average speed of the satellite, in meter per second, in its orbit around the sun?

$$speed = \frac{distance}{time}$$

A) 12,508

B) 25,016

C) 45,028

D) 600,372

$$\frac{1,420,000,000,000 \ m}{1.8 \times 365 \times 24 \times 3,600 \ s} = 25,016 \frac{m}{s}$$

2

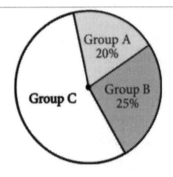

Group A 20%

Group C

Group B 25%

The distribution of student groups in a trip is given above.

If 165 students are from Group C, how many students are from Group A?

A) 60

B) 75

C) 80

D) 100

$100 - (25 + 20) = 55$ 55% Group C

$100 \cdot A \cdot \frac{55}{100} = 165 \cdot 100$ $A = 300$

Group A: $300 \cdot \frac{20}{100} = 60$

3

$$\frac{4}{0.01} + \frac{0.4}{0.04}$$

What is the equivalent of the expression above?

A) 110

B) 114

C) 401

D) 410

$$\frac{4 \times 100}{0.01 \times 100} + \frac{0.4 \times 100}{0.04 \times 100}$$

$$\frac{400}{1} + \frac{40}{4} = 400 + 10 = 410$$

4

	Rock	Pop	Total
Ages 16-17	22	73	95
Ages 17-18	41	44	85
Total	63	117	180

A survey was conducted in the United Kingdom regarding music preferences. Given on the table above is the data of 180 randomly selected teenagers aged 16 to 18.

According to these data, which of the following is the percent that represents those who listen to pop music?

A) 20%

B) 35%

C) 50%

D) 65%

$$\frac{117}{180} = 65\%$$

5

$$\sqrt{4} - \sqrt[3]{-8} + \sqrt{(-2)^4} \div \sqrt[4]{(-4)^2}$$

What is the result of the operation given above?

A) 2

B) 3

C) 4

D) 6

$\sqrt{4} - \sqrt[3]{(-2)^3} + \sqrt{(-2)^4} \div \sqrt[4]{(-4)^2}$

$2 - (-2)^{\frac{3}{3}} + (-2)^{\frac{4}{2}} \div 16^{\frac{1}{4}}$

$2 - (-2) + 4 \div 2^{\frac{4}{4}}$

$4 + 4 \div 2 = 4 + 2 = \boxed{6}$

6

Costs Comparison of Toys		
Toys	Cost at Fred's Toys	Cost at Ann's Toys
Shopkin	$25	$24
Minion	$40	$46
Barbie	$35	$30

If a customer receives a 25% discount from Fred's Toys and a 35% discount from Ann's Toys, how much more would he pay, in dollars, to buy a minion and a shopkin from Fred's Toys than Ann's Toys?

A) $3

B) $3.25

C) $4

D) $4.75

Fred's Toys : $(25+40) \cdot \dfrac{75}{100} = \$48.75$

Ann's Toys : $(24+46) \cdot \dfrac{65}{100} = \$45.50$

$48.75 - 45.50 = \boxed{\$3.25}$

7

If $a - b = 0$ then which of the following should be equivalent to $a + b$?

A) a^2

B) 0

C) $\dfrac{a}{b}$

D) $2b$

$a - b = 0$ $a = b$

$a + b = b + b = \boxed{2b}$

8

Price of Socks in Store A	
Brown	$2 per 5 batches
Black	$3 per 7 batches
Blue	$5 per 9 batches
Orange	$7 per 11 batches

Which color of socks cost the most per batch in Store A?

A) Brown $= \dfrac{\$2}{5} = \$0.40$

B) Blue $= \dfrac{\$3}{7} = \$0.43$

C) Black $= \dfrac{\$5}{9} = \$0.55$

D) Orange $= \dfrac{\$7}{11} = \$0.63$

9

Anthony studied a lot and increased his SAT test score from 1200 to 1500. What is the percent increase of his score?

A) 20

B) 25

C) 30

D) 40

$$\frac{1500-1200}{1200} = \frac{300}{1200} = \frac{1.25}{4.25} = 25\%$$

11

Isotopes	Percent Abundance
24 amu	78.70%
25 amu	10.13%
26 amu	11.17%

Average atomic mass and percent abundances of three isotopes of Magnesium are given in the table above. What is the average mass of magnesium, in amu?

A) 24.3 $\frac{24\cdot(78.70)+25\cdot(10.13)+26\cdot(11.17)}{100}$

B) 24.8 $\frac{1,888.8+253.25+290.42}{100}$

C) 25.2

D) 25.6 $\frac{2,432.47}{100} = 24.3$

10

$$\frac{\sqrt{n}}{4} = 3\sqrt{2}$$

What is the value of n in the equation given above?

A) 24 $\cancel{4}\cdot\frac{\sqrt{n}}{\cancel{4}} = 3\sqrt{2}\cdot 4$ $\left(\sqrt{n}\right)^2 = \left(12\sqrt{2}\right)^2$

B) 72 $n = 144\cdot 2$

C) 288 $n = 288$

D) 576

12

$$\dfrac{1}{\dfrac{1}{x+1}+\dfrac{1}{x+2}}$$

Which of the following is equivalent to the expression above?

A) $\dfrac{x^2+3x+2}{2x+3}$ $\dfrac{1}{\frac{1}{x+1}+\frac{1}{x+2}} = \dfrac{1}{\frac{x+2}{(x+1)(x+2)}+\frac{x+1}{(x+1)(x+2)}}$

B) $2x+3$

C) x^2+3x+2 $\dfrac{1}{\frac{2x+3}{x^2+3x+2}} = \dfrac{x^2+3x+2}{2x+3}$

D) $\dfrac{2x+3}{x^2+3x+2}$

13

Type K trees produce 20% more apples than Type L trees.

Based on this observation, if the Type K trees produced 156 apples, how many apples did the Type L trees produce?

$$\frac{120}{100} \cdot L = K$$

A) 120

B) 130 $\frac{100}{120} \cdot \frac{120}{100} \cdot L = 156 \cdot \frac{100}{120}$

C) 144

D) 168 $L = 130$

14

$$(2^{-2} + 2^{0}) \cdot 5$$

What is the result of the operation given above?

A) 0.25 $\left(2^{-2} + 2^{0}\right) \cdot 5 = \left(\frac{1}{2^{2}} + 1\right) \cdot 5$

B) 1.25

C) 6.25 $= \left(\frac{1}{4} + 1\right) \cdot 5$

D) 20 $= (0.25 + 1) \, 5$

$= 1.25 \cdot 5$

$= 6.25$

15

$$5^{x+2} = \left(\left(\left(\frac{1}{7}\right)^{3}\right)^{0}\right)^{41}$$

What is the value of x that satisfies the equation given above?

A) -3 $5^{x+2} = \left(\frac{1}{7}\right)^{0}$ $5^{x+2} = 1$

B) -2

C) -1 $x+2 = 0$

D) 1 $x = -2$

16

Dominant Color	Large	Small	Total
Green	-	3	10
Blue	6	9	15
Total	-	-	25

Ricardo classified his favorite paintings hanging in an art gallery by both size and dominant color. The results are in the table above. Ricardo found that 40% of his favorite paintings were green.

How many of Ricardo's favorite paintings are small and have blue as the dominant color?

A) 4 $25 \cdot \frac{40}{100} = 10$ Green $25 - 10 = 15$ Blue

B) 6

C) 9 $15 - 6 = 9$ Small Blue

D) 15

17

The square of a positive number is the same as 5 times the number added by 36. What is the square root of that number?

$$x^2 = 5x + 36$$

A) 3

$-5x - 36 \quad -5x - 36$

$$x^2 - 5x - 36 = 0$$

B) 4

$$(x-9)(x+4) = 0$$

C) 9

$x - 9 = 0 \qquad x + 4 = 0$
$+9 \quad +9 \qquad -4 \quad -4$

D) 16

$x = 9 \qquad\qquad x = -4$

$$\sqrt{9} = 3$$

18

$$\sqrt[3]{9^{x-2}} = 81$$

What is the value of x in the equation given above?

$$\sqrt[3]{9^{x-2}} = 81$$

A) 1

$$9^{\frac{x-2}{3}} = 9^2$$

B) 2

C) 4

$\cancel{3} \cdot \dfrac{x-2}{3} = 2 \cdot 3 \qquad x - 2 = 6$

D) 8

$$x = 8$$

19

If $\dfrac{a}{b} = \dfrac{2}{3}$, what is the value of $\dfrac{a+b}{a-b}$?

A) -5   Let $a = 2$, $b = 3$ then;

B) -3

$$\dfrac{2+3}{2-3} = \dfrac{5}{-1} = -5$$

C) -1

D) 5

20

Which of the following lists of numbers is arranged in ASCENDING order?

A) 5913, 5914, 5967, 5975, 5963, 5970, 5976

B) 5808, 5823, 5863, 5886, 5943, 5929, 5924

C) 5813, 5846, 5897, 5901, 5939, 5945, 5996

D) 5808, 5853, 5831, 5907, 5917, 5915, 5927

21

Hamburger (Per Day)				
Student year	0	1	2 or more	Total
Freshman	15	11	11	37
Sophomore	6	22	28	56
Junior	8	9	51	68
Senior	1	4	34	39
Total	30	46	124	200

A survey was conducted among a random sample of students in a high school cafeteria about hamburger consumption. The results per daily consumption are given in the table above.

Which of the following statements is supported by the data given in the table?

Seniors : $\frac{4}{39}$ < Sophomores : $\frac{6}{56}$

A) A higher percentage of seniors than sophomores eat one hamburger.

B) A higher percentage of juniors than freshman eat two or more hamburgers.

C) 60% of all students surveyed eat the hamburger. All students eat hamburger

D) 6% of sophomores do not eat the hamburger.

All sophomores eat hamburger

Juniors : $\frac{51}{68}$ > Freshman : $\frac{11}{37}$

22

3 scruples = 1dram
3 drams = 1ounce
12 ounces = 1pound

Based on the information given in the table above, if you use 45 scruples of a medicine per day for 12 days, this will be how much total medicine in pounds?

A) 5 $\frac{3\ scruples}{1\ dram} \cdot \frac{3\ dram}{1\ ounce} \cdot \frac{12\ ounce}{1\ pound} = \frac{108\ scruples}{1\ pound}$

B) 12

C) 60 $12 \cdot 45\ scruples \cdot \frac{1\ pound}{108\ scruples} = 5\ pound$

D) 75

23

$$\frac{m}{n} = 3 \qquad 15\frac{n}{m} = A$$

What is the value of A?

A) 5

B) 18

C) 45

D) 60

$\frac{m}{n} = \frac{3}{1}$, then $\frac{n}{m} = \frac{1}{3}$,

$15\frac{n}{m} = 15 \cdot \frac{1}{3} = 5$

24

$$\sqrt{0.09} - \sqrt{0.16} + \sqrt{0.49}$$

What is the result of the operation given above?

A) 0.2

B) 0.4

C) 0.6

D) 0.8

$\sqrt{\frac{9}{100}} - \sqrt{\frac{16}{100}} + \sqrt{\frac{49}{100}}$

$\frac{3}{10} - \frac{4}{10} + \frac{7}{10} = \frac{6}{10} = 0.6$

25

People are standing in a line to get on the bus. As Edison stood in the line, he noticed that there are 9 more people behind him than there is in front of him. If the total number of people in the line is 3 times the number of people in front of him, then how many of the people in the line are behind Edison?

A) 9

B) 10

C) 19

D) 30

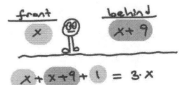

$$front \qquad behind$$
$$x \qquad x+9$$

$x + x + 9 + 1 = 3 \cdot x$

$2x + 10 = 3x$
$\quad -2x \qquad -2x$
$\qquad x = 10$

$x + 9 = 19$

CONTINUE ▶

$$\begin{array}{r} 75 \\ 24\overline{)1,804} \\ \underline{168} \\ 124 \\ \underline{120} \\ 4 \end{array}$$

Manuella turned on her computer, checked in for her flight and left home to go to the airport. She forgot to turn off the computer while she was leaving home and the computer was on for 24 hours a day for 1,804 hours. Manuella did the work above to determine how many days the computer was on.

Manuella needs to finish the calculation to find how long, in days, the computer was on. Which statement about Manuella's calculations is true?

A) Manuella can complete the calculation by adding on 0.4 of a day since the remainder is 4 and found that the computer was on for 75.4 days.

B) Manuella can complete the calculation by dividing 24 ÷ 4 to get 6 and found that the computer was on for 75.6 days

C) Manuella can complete the calculation by dividing 4 ÷ 24 to get 0.16 and found that the computer was on for 75.16 days.

D) Manuella can complete the calculation by subtracting 24 – 4 to get 20 and found that the computer was on for 75.20 days.

4 is not divisible by 24 but Manuella can add a zero next to 4, make it 40 and continue division so that she gets 75.16

A baseball team won *a* games and lost *b* games. What part of its games did it loss?

A) $\dfrac{a}{a+b}$

B) $\dfrac{b}{a+b}$

C) $\dfrac{a+b}{a}$

D) $\dfrac{a-b}{a}$

Games lost = b
Total number of games = a+b

$\dfrac{b}{a+b}$ *of the games is lost.*

28

$$\frac{2x}{x+3} \div \frac{12}{3x+9}$$

Which of the following is equivalent to the expression above given that $x \neq -3$?

A) $\frac{x}{2}$

B) $2x$

C) $3x$

D) $8x$

$\frac{2x}{x+3} \div \frac{12}{3x+9} = \frac{2x}{x+3} \cdot \frac{3x+9}{12}$

$= \frac{2x}{x+3} \cdot \frac{3(x+3)}{12\,4}$

$= \frac{2x}{4} = \frac{x}{2}$

29

The Environmental Protection Agency (EPA) identifies contaminants to regulate in drinking water. According to the drinking water regulations of EPA, the maximum amount of nitrate that can be present in water is 15 milligrams per liter. A scientist is measuring the amount of nitrate in a local lake to see if it is safe to drink. The scientist takes a sample of 25 liters of water. If the number of milligrams per liter of nitrate in the lake water is 40% of the maximum value that is safe to drink, how many grams of nitrate should the scientist expect to find in her sample?

$\frac{15mg}{1\!\!\!\;L} \cdot 25L \cdot \frac{40}{100} = 150mg = 0.15g$

A) 0.15 g

B) 0.375 g

C) 6 g

D) 15 g

30

$$2x = y = 7z$$
$$2x + y + 7z = 42$$

What is the value of $x + y + z$?

A) 20

B) 21

C) 22

D) 23

$2x = y = 7z = k$ $\frac{14}{2} = \frac{2x}{2}$ $x=7$

$2x + y + 7z = 42$ $14 = y$

$k + k + k = 42$

$\frac{3k}{3} = \frac{42}{3}$ $\frac{14}{7} = \frac{7z}{7}$ $z = 2$

$k = 14$ $x+y+z = 7+14+2 = 23$

31

$$\frac{a}{b} = \frac{c}{d}$$

Based on the equality above, which of the following expression is true?

A) $\frac{a-b}{b} = \frac{c+d}{d}$

B) $\frac{a-d}{b} = \frac{c-b}{a}$

C) $\frac{a+c}{c} = \frac{c+d}{b}$

D) $\frac{c+d}{c} = \frac{a+b}{a}$

$\frac{c}{c} + \frac{d}{c} = \frac{a}{a} + \frac{b}{a}$

$1 + \frac{d}{c} = 1 + \frac{b}{a}$

$\frac{d}{c} = \frac{b}{a}$

33

If buying n pizzas cost p dollars, then how much will it cost to buy m pizzas at the same rate?

A) $\dfrac{pm}{n}$ $\dfrac{p}{n}$ = cost of 1 pizza.

B) $\dfrac{m}{pn}$ m pizza will cost $\dfrac{m \cdot p}{n}$

C) mpn

D) $\dfrac{mn}{p}$

34

I. $\dfrac{a}{a+b}$ II. $\dfrac{b}{a+b}$ III. $\dfrac{a+b}{a}$ IV. $\dfrac{a-b}{a}$

A baseball team won a games and lost b games. What part of its games did it lose?

A) I $\dfrac{\text{game lost}}{\text{total games}} = \dfrac{b}{a+b}$

B) II

C) III

D) IV

35

If $\dfrac{x-1}{3} = k$ and $k = 3$, what is the value of x?

A) 2 $3k = x-1$

B) 4 $3 \cdot 3 = x-1$

C) 9 $9 = x-1$

D) 10 $x = 10$

36

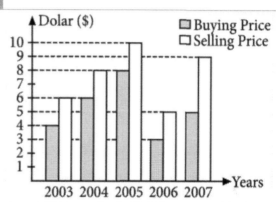

The column chart given above shows the buying and selling prices of items sold in a store between 2003 and 2007.

How many percents is the profit margin of the store in 2007?

A) 40   In 2007, buying price is $5 and

B) 50   selling price is $9. Profit is $4

C) 80   out of $5. So %;

D) 90 $\dfrac{4}{5} = 80\%$

37

Four years ago, Nathaniel bought a car for $9,300 which is now worth $5,700.

What is the percentage of depreciation of his car?

A) 38%

B) 38.7%

C) 59.3%

D) 63.15%

$$\frac{9,300 - 5,700}{9,300} = \frac{3,600}{9,300}$$

$$= 38.7\%$$

38

A lemonade mixture calls for a 75% pure water and 25% lemon extract. How many glasses of water must be added to a 4 glasses of lemon extract to make the lemonade mixture?

A) 7.5

B) 8

C) 12

D) 20

75 water, 25 lemon extract.

3 water, 1 lemon extract.

$$\frac{?}{3 \cdot 4} \quad \frac{4}{"} \quad ^{"}$$

$3 \cdot 4 = ? \cdot 1 \quad \boxed{? = 12}$

39

A	K	O	R	Z
1	2	3	4	5

Which of the following choices contains the letters add up to 9 after they are converted to numbers?

A) K, R, Z $2 + 4 + 5 = 11$

B) O, A, R $3 + 1 + 4 = 8$

C) O, R, Z $3 + 4 + 5 = 8$

D) A, O, Z $1 + 3 + 5 = 9$

40

In a book store books cost $18 each and notebooks cost $10 each. Sera buys n books, b notebooks and pays D dollars Which of the following equation represents for the number of notebooks bought?

A) $\dfrac{D+18n}{10}$

B) $\dfrac{D-18n}{10}$

C) $\dfrac{18n-D}{10}$

D) $\dfrac{D-10n}{18}$

$n \cdot 18 + b \cdot 10 = D$
$-18n \qquad\qquad -18n$

$\dfrac{10b}{10} = \dfrac{D-18n}{10}$

$\boxed{b = \dfrac{D-18n}{10}}$

41

Stephanie does push-ups and sit-ups every morning. She does p push-ups and 2p+5 sit-ups.

2p+5 means 5 more than two times

Which statement describes the number of sit-ups Stephanie does every morning?

A) The number of sit-ups is 5 more than half the number of push-ups she does.

B) The number of sit-ups is 5 fewer than half the number of push-ups she does.

C) The number of sit-ups is 5 more than twice the number of push-ups she does

D) The number of sit-ups is 5 fewer than twice the number of push-ups she does.

42

A fruit salad is made from bananas, pears and strawberries mixed in the ratio of 2 to 5 to 3 respectively by weight. What fraction of the mixture by weight is pears?

A) $\frac{1}{2}$

B) $\frac{2}{3}$

C) $\frac{3}{5}$

D) $\frac{3}{10}$

$b : p : s = 2 : 5 : 3$

$\frac{5}{2+5+3} = \frac{5}{10} = \frac{1}{2}$

43

The length of one piece of pipe is 6 inches more than three times the length of a shorter section. If the length of the longer pipe is 33 inches, what is the length, in inches, of the shorter pipe?

A) 9

B) 10

C) 11

D) 13

Let shorter pipe $= s$

Longer pipe $= 3s + 6$

$33 = 3s + 6$

$-6 \qquad -6$

$\frac{27}{3} = \frac{3s}{3}$

$s = 9$

44

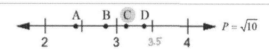

Use the number line given above to answer the following question.

Which point on the number line is the best approximation for P?

A) Point A

B) Point B

C) Point C

D) Point D

$\sqrt{9} < \sqrt{10}$

$3 < \sqrt{10}$

P is slightly bigger than 3, which is C.

CONTINUE ▶

45

Age (years)	Male	Female	Total
0-20	54	70	124
21-40	94	86	180
41-65	114	142	256
65+	88	102	190
Total	350	400	750

The age and gender distribution of a random sample of people from a population is given in the table above. If the whole population consists of 12,000 people, which of the following statements is true?

A) It is expected that there are 6,400 males in the population.

B) It is expected that there will be 1,824 females between 41 and 65 years old in the population. $\frac{86}{750} \times 12,000 = 1,376$

C) It is expected that there will be 1,376 females between 21 and 40 years old in the population.

D) The number of males in the population can not be estimated with the information given.

46

$$-1 < \bar{a} < 0 < \overset{+}{b} < 1$$

Which of the following is NOT true?

A) $b^2 < b$ Let $a = -\frac{1}{2}$ and $b = \frac{1}{2}$ and
B) $a^2 > a$ try each option.
C) $a^3 < a$ $\left(-\frac{1}{2}\right)^3 < -\frac{1}{2}$
D) $b^3 > a^3$ $-\frac{1}{8} < -\frac{1}{2}$ (not correct)

47

If $2r = 3k$ and $5k = 7p$, then find p in terms of r?

A) $\frac{10}{21}r$ $\frac{2r}{3} = \frac{3k}{3}$ $5k = 7p$

B) $\frac{21}{10}r$ $k = \frac{2}{3}r$ $\frac{5}{7} \cdot \frac{2}{3}r = \frac{7p}{7}$

C) $\frac{2}{7}r$ $p = \frac{10}{21}r$

D) $\frac{2}{15}r$

48

In a class of 56 students 37 are taking Statistics, 29 are taking Calculus. Of the students taking Statistics or Calculus, 11 are taking both courses. How many students are NOT enrolled in either course?

A) 1

B) 11

C) 18

D) 44

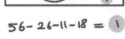

$56 - 26 - 11 - 18 = 1$

49

If $2^{10} = a$, then what is the equivalent of $2^{10} + 2^{11}$ in terms of a?

A) $2a$

B) $3a$

C) $11a$

D) $21a$

[handwritten work]
$2^{10} + 2^{11} = 2^{10} + 2^{10+1} = 2^{10} + 2^{10} \cdot 2^1$
$= 2^{10}(1 + 2^1)$
$= 2^{10} \cdot 3$
$= 3a$

52

A is 25% of B and C is 10% of B. What percentage of C is A?

A) 15

B) 25

C) 35

D) 250

[handwritten work]
$\frac{25}{100} \cdot B = A$
$\frac{10}{100} B = C \cdot 10$
$B = 10C$
$\frac{25}{100} \cdot 10C = A$
$\frac{250}{100} \cdot C = A$ A is 250% of C

50

$\overset{+}{5A} = \overset{+}{3B}$ $\dfrac{4}{B+} = \dfrac{C-}{3}$ $\dfrac{C-}{D-} = 5$

[handwritten] A-B: directly   B-C: inversely   C-D: directly

Based on the relations given above, which of the following statements is not true?

A) A and B are directly proportional.

B) B and C are inversely proportional.

C) A and C are inversely proportional.

D) A and D are directly proportional.

[handwritten] A-C: inversely, C-D directly proportional, so;
A-D are inversely proportional.

53

$$5x - 9 \ge 6x - 7$$

Which of the following numbers is not a solution of the inequality given above?

A) -1

B) -3

C) -4

D) -5

[handwritten work]
$5x - 9 \ge 6x - 7$
$-5x + 7 \qquad -5x + 7$
$-2 \ge x$

[number line showing ...-4, -3, -2, -1, 0 with point at -2 and -1 circled]

51

Which comparison is true?

A) $8.5 < \sqrt{18} < 9.5$

B) $17 < \sqrt{18} < 19$

C) $4 < \sqrt{18} < 4.5$

D) $4.5 < \sqrt{18} < 5$

[handwritten work]
$\sqrt{18} > \sqrt{16} \Rightarrow \sqrt{18} > 4$
$4.5^2 = 20.25$
$\sqrt{16} < \sqrt{18} < \sqrt{20.25}$
$4 < \sqrt{18} < 4.5$

54

The expression $\dfrac{3x-4}{x+2}$ is equivalent to which of the following?

A) $3 - \dfrac{10}{x+2}$

B) $3 + \dfrac{2}{x+2}$

C) $3 + \dfrac{10}{x+2}$

D) $3 - \dfrac{2}{x+2}$

[handwritten long division]
$x+2 \overline{)\ 3x - 4}$ quotient 3
$\quad \underline{-3x + 6}$
$\quad\quad -10$

$\dfrac{3x-4}{x+2} = 3 + \dfrac{-10}{x+2}$

55

If the school is 12 miles away from Anne's house and Starbucks is 4 miles away from the school, which of the following conclusions must be true?

A) Starbucks is exactly 8 miles from Anne's house.

B) Anne's house is closer to the school than Starbucks.

C) Anne's house is east of the school.

D) Anne's house is at most 16 miles from Starbucks.

House
Starbucks can be at least 4, at most 12 mile away.

56

A specific DNA sequencing machine can identify the sequence of base pairs of a DNA, taking approximately 10 seconds to sequence 1000 base pairs.

If a researcher wants to sequence a gene made up of 150,000 base pairs, how many minutes would it take for him to get the sequences?

A) 25

B) 60

C) 150

D) 1500

$$\frac{150,000}{1,000} = 150 \quad 150 \times 10 = 1,500\,s$$

$$\frac{1,500}{60} = 25\,minutes$$

57

If $\dfrac{a+b}{a} = 6$ then what is $\dfrac{a+b}{b}$?

A) $\dfrac{8}{7}$

B) $\dfrac{6}{5}$

C) $\dfrac{4}{3}$

D) $\dfrac{3}{2}$

$$6a = a+b$$
$$5a = b$$

$$\frac{a+5a}{5a} = \frac{6a}{5a} = \frac{6}{5}$$

58

If is $12 + 3x$ is 11 less than 36, what is the value of $12x$?

A) 52

B) 140

C) 148

D) 236

$$12 + 3x = 36 - 11$$
$$4 \cdot 3x = 13 \cdot 4$$
$$12x = 52$$

Do not solve for x, solve for 12x.

59

Michael leaves his house and bikes south at a constant speed of 8 miles per hour. His dad, John, leaves the same house three hours later, driving south at a constant speed of 12 miles per hour.

How long will it take for dad, John, in hours, to reach the son, Michael?

A) 2

B) 3

C) 4

D) 6

In three hours Michael travels 3×8 = 24 miles. Every hour John approaches Michael by 12−8 = 4 miles. It will take 24 ÷ 4 = 6 hours for John to reach Michael.

60

An office has two stapling machines. Machine K staples a batch of paper in 12 hours and Machine L staples same batch of paper in 3 hours. How long would it take to staple 5 batch of paper if two machines work together?

A) 2.4

B) 5

C) 12

D) 17

K staples $\frac{1}{12}$ in one hour

L   " $\frac{1}{3}$ "   "

K and L staples $\frac{1}{12} + \frac{1}{3}$ of one batch in one hour

$$\left(\frac{1}{12} + \frac{1}{3}\right) \cdot t = 5$$

$$\frac{12}{5} \cdot \frac{5}{12} t = 5 \cdot \frac{12}{5} \qquad t = 12$$

61

$$5^{-2} + 5^{-1} + 5 = N$$

What is the value of N given above?

A) -10

B) 25

C) 5.24

D) 0.24

$$5^{-2} + 5^{-1} + 5 = N$$

$$\frac{1}{5^2} + \frac{1}{5} + 5 = N$$

$$\frac{4 \cdot 1}{4 \cdot 25} + \frac{20 \cdot 1}{20 \cdot 5} + 5 = N$$

$$\frac{4}{100} + \frac{20}{100} + 5 = N$$

$$0.04 + 0.20 + 5 = N$$

$$5.24 = N$$

62

A piece of cloth which is 75cm long and 32m wide can be produced with 15kg of cotton.

How many meters wide of cloth that is 80cm long can be produced with 12kg of cotton?

A) 12

B) 24

C) 36

D) 96

$$\frac{15kg}{75 \cdot 32} = \frac{12}{80 \cdot x}$$

$$\frac{15 \cdot 80 \cdot x}{15 \cdot 80} = \frac{75 \cdot 32 \cdot 12}{15 \cdot 80}$$

$$x = \frac{5 \cdot 32 \cdot 12}{80} = 2 \cdot 12 = 24$$

63

On a map, 1 centimeter represents 8 kilometers. What area is represented by a square on the map with a perimeter of 24 centimeters?

A) 48 square kilometers

B) 192 square kilometers

C) 2,304 square kilometers

D) 36,864 square kilometers

6cm, 6cm, 6cm, 6cm (square diagram)

1 cm — 8 km
6 cm — x km
x = 48 km

Area = 48 × 48 = 2,304 square kilometers

64

In November, the price of GSM Controlled Automatic Cooking Machine was $150. In December the price increased by 12 percent. During a sale in January, the December price was discounted by 14 percent.

What was the price of the item during the sale in January?

After 12% increase it is 112%
After 14% discount it is 86%

A) $144.48

B) $148

C) $150.48

D) $162

$150 · $\frac{112}{100}$ · $\frac{86}{100}$ = $144.48

65

$$\frac{1 - \dfrac{1}{x}}{1 + \dfrac{1}{x}} = \frac{3}{1}$$

What is the value of x?

First you do criss cross multiplication

A) -3

B) -2

C) -1

D) 1

$3 + \frac{3}{x} = 1 - \frac{1}{x}$

$+\frac{1}{x}$ $-3 + \frac{x}{x}$

$\frac{4}{x} = -2$

$\frac{4}{-2} = \frac{-2x}{-2}$ x = -2

66

The price of 500mg L-Ribose is $18. L-Ribose is cretaed with 90% purity. If a customer orders $90 of L-Ribose, it will contain what amount of pure L-Ribose?

A) 0.25g

B) 2.25g

C) 2.5g

D) 2.75g

$\frac{90}{18} = 5$ 5 × 500 = 2,500mg

2,500 × $\frac{90}{100}$ = 2,250mg

2.25 g

67

$$a = \frac{7.2b^3}{c^2}$$

The relation between a, b and c is given above. What happens to a when both b and c are doubled?

A) Halved
B) Doubled
C) Quadrupled
D) Multiplied by 8

$$\frac{7.2(2b)^3}{(2c)^2} = \frac{7.2 \cdot 8 b^3}{4 \; c^2}$$

$$= 2 \cdot \frac{7.2 \, b^3}{c^2}$$

It is doubled.

68

Mae fed $\frac{1}{11}$ of the ducks at a farm. Which decimal is equal to the fraction of ducks Mae fed?

A) $0.\overline{01}$
B) $0.0\overline{1}$
C) $0.\overline{09}$
D) $0.0\overline{9}$

$$0.0909 = 0.\overline{09}$$

$$11 \overline{)\,100}$$
$$\underline{-99}$$
$$100$$
$$\underline{-99}$$
$$1$$

69

Isabel has some coins in her pocket consisting of dimes, nickels, and pennies. She has three more nickels than dimes and two times as many pennies as nickels.

If the total value of the coins is 72 cents, how many nickels does she have?

A) 3
B) 4
C) 6
D) 8

¢10	¢5	¢1
dimes	nickels	pennies
d	d+3	2(d+3)

$$10d + 5(d+3) + 2(d+3)\cdot 1 = 72$$
$$10d + 5d+15 + 2d+6 = 72$$
$$17d + 21 = 72$$
$$-21 \quad -21$$
$$\frac{17d}{17} = \frac{51}{17} \quad d=3$$
$$d+3 = 6$$

70

Alicia is a student at Ridgewood High School. She surveyed a random sample of the sophomore class of his high school to determine whether the Spring Festival should be held in April or May. Of the 80 students surveyed, 30% preferred April and the rest preferred May.

According to this information, about how many students in the entire 240 person class would be expected to prefer having the Spring Festival in May?

A) 56
B) 72
C) 96
D) 168

If 30% preferred April, then 70% prefers May.

$$\frac{70}{100} \cdot 240 = 168 \text{ students are expected to prefer having it in May.}$$

71

Harris wants to divide number N by 6, but, by mistake, he pushes 8 button of the calculator instead of 6 and gets a result which is 10 less than the correct answer. Which of the following equations determine N?

A) $\dfrac{N+10}{8}$

B) $\dfrac{N}{8} - \dfrac{N}{6} = 10$

C) $\dfrac{N}{8} + 10 = \dfrac{N}{6}$

D) $\dfrac{N}{6} + \dfrac{N}{8} = 10$

Correct division $= \dfrac{N}{6}$

Wrong division $= \dfrac{N}{8}$

$\dfrac{N}{8} = \dfrac{N}{6} - 10$

$\dfrac{N}{8} + 10 = \dfrac{N}{6}$

72

If the sum of two consecutive integers is 17, what is their product?

A) 30
B) 48
C) 56
D) 72

If integers are x and $x+1$, then:
$x + (x+1) = 17$
$2x + 1 = 17$
$2x = 16$
$x = 8$
$8 \cdot 9 = 72$

73

A rectangle was altered by changing its length and width. Its length is increased by 20 percent and its width is decreased by k percent. If these alterations increased the area of the rectangle by 8 percent, what is the value of k?

A) 8
B) 10
C) 15
D) 20

$\dfrac{120}{100} \ell \cdot \dfrac{100-k}{100} w = \dfrac{108}{100} \ell w$

$\dfrac{120 \cdot (100-k)}{100 \cdot 100} = \dfrac{108}{100}$

$100 - k = 90$
$-k = -10$
$k = 10$

74

The price of an antique increased by 20% but is then decreased by 20%.

Which of the following is the overall change of the initial price?

A) No change
B) Reduced by 20%
C) Raised by 4%
D) Reduced by 4%

After 20% increase it will be 120%
After 20% decrease it will be 80%

$P \cdot \dfrac{120}{100} \cdot \dfrac{80}{100} = P \cdot \dfrac{96}{100}$

Reduced by 4%

CONTINUE ▶

75

If $\dfrac{a}{3} = \dfrac{b}{5}$ then what is $\dfrac{ab+a^2}{a^2+b^2}$?

A) $\dfrac{17}{20}$

B) $\dfrac{12}{17}$

C) $\dfrac{5}{34}$

D) $\dfrac{8}{34}$

You can let $a=3$, $b=5$. Then;

$\dfrac{3 \cdot 5 + 3^2}{3^2 + 5^2} = \dfrac{15+9}{9+25} = \dfrac{24}{34} = \boxed{\dfrac{12}{17}}$

76

When a ball bounces it reaches three-fourths of its previous height with each bounce.

How high was the ball when it was dropped if it reached a hight of 54 cm after the third bounce?

A) 72

B) 96

C) 128

D) 256

$H \cdot \dfrac{3}{4} \cdot \dfrac{3}{4} \cdot \dfrac{3}{4} = 54$

$\dfrac{64}{27} \cdot H \cdot \dfrac{27}{64} = 54 \cdot \dfrac{64}{27}$

$\boxed{H = 128}$

77

Two numbers differing by 4 has a sum of m. What is the value of the bigger number in terms of m?

A) $\dfrac{m-4}{2}$

B) $m-4$

C) $\dfrac{m-4}{2} + 4$

D) $\dfrac{m-4}{2} - 4$

bigger　smaller　sum

$\underline{\quad x \quad} + \underline{\quad x-4 \quad} = \underline{\quad m \quad}$

$2x - 4 = m$
$\quad\quad +4 \quad +4$

$\dfrac{2x}{2} = \dfrac{m+4}{2}$

$\boxed{x = \dfrac{m+4}{2}}$

$\dfrac{m-4}{2} + \dfrac{4 \cdot 2}{2} = \dfrac{m-4+8}{2} = \dfrac{m+4}{2}$

78

$$m(x+3) = 2x - m + 1$$

For which value of m does the equation above have no solution?

A) -4

B) -1

C) 2

D) 3

$mx + 3m = 2x - m + 1$

When $m=2$ then x terms are eliminated, there will be no solution.

79

I. $\dfrac{AB}{12C}$　II. $12\dfrac{AC}{B}$　III. $\dfrac{12C}{AB}$　IV. $\dfrac{BC}{A}$

A dozen apples cost a total of B dollars. At this rate, which of the equations given above can be used to find the number of apples that can be bought for C dollars?

A) I

B) II

C) III

D) IV

1 dozen has 12 items

$\dfrac{12 \cdot A}{12A} = \dfrac{\$B}{12A}$　$\dfrac{\$B}{12A}$ is the price for one apple.

$\dfrac{C}{\frac{B}{12A}} = C \cdot \dfrac{12A}{B} = \boxed{\dfrac{12 \, AC}{B}}$

80

If the sum of two integers is 20, which of the following cannot be their product?

$a+b = 20$

A) -125　If $a=-25$ and $b=5$, then $a \cdot b = -125$

B) -21　If $a=-21$ and $b=1$, then $a \cdot b = -21$

C) 19　If $a=19$ and $b=1$, then $a \cdot b = 19$

D) 80　There is no value for $a+b=20$, and $a \cdot b = 80$

TEST DIRECTION

DIRECTIONS

Read the questions carefully and then choose the ONE best answer to each question.

Be sure to allocate your time carefully so you are able to complete the entire test within the testing session. You may go back and review your answers at any time.

You may use any available space in your test booklet for scratch work.

Questions in this booklet are not actual test questions but they are the samples for commonly asked questions.

This test aims to cover all topics which may appear on the actual test. However some topics may not be covered.

Studying this booklet will be preparing you for the actual test. It will not guarantee improving your test score but it will help you pass your exam on the first attempt.

Some useful tips for answering multiple choice questions;

- Start with the questions that you can easily answer.

- Underline the keywords in the question.

- Be sure to read all the choices given.

- Watch for keywords such as NOT, always, only, all, never, completely.

- Do not forget to answer every question.

1

$$f(x) = \sqrt{x^2 + 16}$$

Which of the following is the domain of the function given above?

A) All real numbers greater than -16.
B) All real numbers greater than -4.
C) All real numbers greater than 4.
D) All real numbers.

2

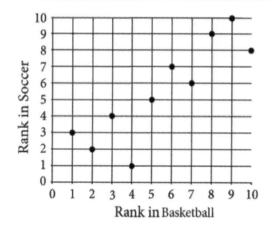

Rank in Soccer (y-axis)
Rank in Basketball (x-axis)

The ranking of 10 students in two sports is shown above in the scatter plot. How many students received a better rank in Soccer than Basketball?

A) 2
B) 3
C) 4
D) 5

3

$$K@L = 3K - 2L$$

According to the operation defined above, what is the value of (M@N) @P?

A) 3M - 2N +3P
B) 3M - 2N - 2P
C) 9M - 6N - 2P
D) 3M + 3N - 2P

4

$$-6 < x < 4$$

$$-2 < y < 11$$

If both x and y are integers, what is the minimum integer value of $3x - 5y$?

A) -65
B) -73
C) -74
D) -76

5

$$3x = \frac{1}{4}y - 2$$

In the *xy*-plane, which of the following best describes the graph of the equation given above?

A) It has a negative x-intercept and positive slope.

B) It has positive y-intercept and positve slope.

C) It has positive x-intercept and positive y-intercept.

D) It has a negative slope and postive a negative y-intercept.

6

Hena wants to make a scatter plot comparing the life expectancy, represented in the *y*-axis, and the air pollution, given in the *x*-axis.

Which line fits best for Hena's expectation about her scatter plot?

A) A vertical line

B) A negative slope line

C) A positive slope line

D) A horizontal line

7

$$y = x^2 - 24$$
$$y = x - 12$$

Which ordered pair is a solution of the system of equations given above?

A) (4,8)

B) (4,−8)

C) (2,−10)

D) (12,0)

8

$$(-x^2 + 3x + 7)(6x^5 - 3x^4 + x^2 + 2x - 5)$$

After the multiplication of the polynomials given above, what will be the coefficent of the term x^3?

A) -2

B) 1

C) 3

D) 5

9

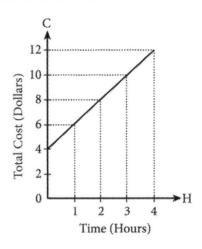

Time (Hours)

The graph above displays the total cost (C) in dollars of renting a toy car for (H) hours. Which of the following is true?

A) C - intercept is the hourly price of renting.

B) The slope of the graph is the initial price of renting.

C) C = 4 + 2H is the relationship between C and H

D) Hourly price for renting is $4

10

$$E = mc^2$$

In physics, mass–energy equivalence is a concept formulated by Albert Einstein that explains the relationship between mass and energy. Which of the following expresses speed of light c in terms of mass and energy ?

A) $c = \dfrac{E}{m}$

B) $c = \sqrt{\dfrac{E}{m}}$

C) $c = \sqrt{E - m}$

D) $c = \dfrac{E}{2m}$

q	$N(q)$
0	1400
1	2800
2	5600
3	11200
4	22400

The relationship netween $N(q)$ and q is defined in the chart above. Which of the following equations best describes this relationship?

A) $N(q) = 1400 \times (2)^q$

B) $N(q) = 1400 \times 2q$

C) $N(q) = 1400 \times 2q^2$

D) $N(q) = 1400 \times q^2$

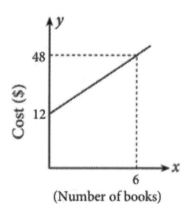

(Number of books)

The graph above shows the cost of the books in a book fair. Which of the following statements is NOT correct?

A) You should pay an entrance fee even if you don't buy any book.

B) The slope of the line gives the price of one book.

C) Entrance fee for the book fair is $12.

D) If you buy 3 books you will pay $24.

13

$$4m - 4 \leq 0$$

Based on the inequality given above, what is the greatest possible value of $5m + 2$?

A) 2

B) 3

C) 5

D) 7

15

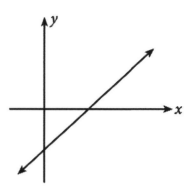

Which of the following statements about the line is true?

A) The slope of the line is negative.

B) y-intercept of the line is positive.

C) x-intercept of the line is negative.

D) $3x - 4y + 10 = 0$ can be the line equation.

14

In 2012, the number of cell phone subscribers in the small town of Molnar were 1,500. The number of subscribers increased by 60% per year after 2012. How many cell phone subscribers were in Molnar in 2015?

A) 1,800

B) 2,400

C) 3,840

D) 6,144

16

$$f(x) = \frac{3}{4}x - 12$$

For the function given above, what domain value corresponds to the range value of 24?

A) 6

B) 27

C) 36

D) 48

17

$$0 < 1 - \frac{2a}{5} \leq \frac{3}{5}$$

Which value below is NOT possible for a ?

A) 1
B) 1.5
C) 2
D) 2.5

18

$$y = 2x^2 + 1$$
$$y = 2x + 5$$

What values of x satisfy the system of equations given above?

A) -1 and 2
B) -1 and 3
C) 2 and 1
D) 0 and 2

19

$$PV = nRT$$

Ideal gas law is given above. How can you express temperature, T, in terms of other variables?

A) $PVnR$

B) $\dfrac{PV}{nR}$

C) $PV + nR$

D) $PV - nR$

20

$$P(t) = P_0 \left(1 + \frac{r}{100}\right)^n$$

The formula given above models the population of a city n years after an initial population of P_0 people is counted. The population grows at a constant rate of $r\%$ per year. The population of the city was 860,000 in 2010. Assume the population grows at a constant rate of 4% per year. According to this formula, which of the following is an expression for the population of the city in the year 2020?

A) $860,000(4)^{10}$

B) $860,000(1.04)^{10}$

C) $(860,000 \times 0.6)^{10}$

D) $(860,000 \times 1.04)^{10}$

21

$$3x^2 + y^2 = 76$$

Based on the equation given above, which of the following is a possible value for y if both x and y are integers?

A) -5

B) -1

C) 0

D) 5

22

$$f(x) = \frac{23}{x+2}$$

What is the range of $f(x)$ if it is defined on all real numbers except -2?

A) All real numbers

B) All real numbers except -3

C) All real numbers except -2

D) All real numbers greater than -2

23

$$a < 0 < b < c$$

Based on the given expression;

  I. $a + c > 0$

  II. $a^2 < b^2$

  III. $ab > ac$

which of the inequalities are always true?

A) Only III

B) Only II

C) I and III

D) II and III

24

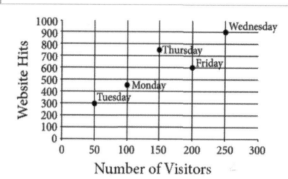

The graph given above shows the number of visitors and website hits. On which day is the ratio of website hits to the number of visitors the smallest?

A) Monday

B) Tuesday

C) Wednesday

D) Friday

25

$$(2a^2 - 3ab - 1) - (3a^2 - 5ab - 4)$$

Which of the following is equivalent to the expression above?

A) $-a^2 + 2ab - 5$
B) $-a^2 - 8ab - 5$
C) $5a^2 - 8ab - 5$
D) $-a^2 + 2ab + 3$

26

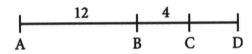

In the figure above AB=12, BC=4 and AD=3CD. What is the value of $\dfrac{BD}{BC}$?

A) 3
B) 4
C) 6
D) 8

27

In a Research Center in Massachusetts, biologists are working on a project about DNA sequencing. In DNA sequencing, it costs approximately 20 cents to sequence 500 base pairs.

If a researcher would like to sequence a gene consisting of 60,000 base pairs, how much would it cost to obtain the sequence?

A) $12
B) $16
C) $24
D) $48

28

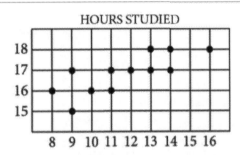

The scatter plot given above shows the number of hours, between 15 and 18, studied by 12 students of various ages, between 8 and 16, at after-school study program.

Which of the following is NOT true, according to this scatter plot?

A) More than half of the students studied more than 16 hours.
B) Four students studied exactly 17 hours.
C) One 12 years old student studied 17 hours.
D) Most of the students were over 9 years old.

CONTINUE ▶

29

$f(x) = \sqrt{x+3}$ for all values $x \geq 0$

$f(x) = x^2 + 5$ for all values of $x < 0$

Given the function above, what is the value of $f(-4) - f(13)$?

A) 17
B) 21
C) 25
D) 173

30

$P(x) = 7x^4 - 3x^3 + 5x + 3$

$Q(x) = -4x^4 - 2x^3 - x^2 - 3x + 4$

Polynomials $P(x)$ and $Q(x)$ are given above. Find the polynomial $2P(x) - 3Q(x)$.

A) $26x^4 + 3x^2 + 19x - 6$
B) $26x^4 + 3x^2 + 13x + 18$
C) $13x^4 - 4x^3 - 2x^2 - 6x + 17$
D) $2x^4 - 12x^3 - 3x^2 + x - 6$

31

The graph above shows the distance of Sam from his home during the particular hours of a day.

Which of the expressions below can NOT be a correct information based on this graph?

A) Sam returns back to his home at 6pm.
B) Sam's Office is 10 miles away from his house.
C) Sam went to the hospital, stayed there 8 hours.
D) Between 8am and 6pm Sam stayed at home.

32

A = {@, #, &}

B = {@, #, !}

Which of the following is a function defined from A to B?

A) { (@, @), (@, #), (@, !)}
B) { (@, @), (#, #), (!, !)}
C) { (@, @), (#, #), (&, @)}
D) { (@, @), (#, !), (@, &)}

33

$$y = (m-3)x^2 - mx + 11$$

If the vertex of the parabola is on (2,7), what is the value of m?

A) 2
B) 3
C) 4
D) 6

34

If you add 3 to the numerator of $\dfrac{a}{b}$, how much the value of $\dfrac{a}{b}$ increases?

A) 3
B) $3a$
C) $\dfrac{3}{a}$
D) $\dfrac{3}{b}$

35

$$P = 240 - 15d$$

Adam wants to sell all the products in his store. The number of products in the store as a function of d is estimated with the equation given above. In the equation P is the number of products left in the store and d is the number of days the store is open.

What is the meaning of the value 15 in this equation?

A) The number of products that are sold per day
B) The number of days to sell all the products in the store
C) The rate of increase of products per day
D) The number of products left in the store at the end of each day

CONTINUE ▶

36

$$A\&B=\frac{A}{B}+A \cdot B$$

If A = 8 and B = -2, what is the value of A&B?

A) -20
B) -12
C) 16
D) 20

37

Which of the following for is true for a line in the xy-plane that has the equation $x=5$?

A) The point (5,-1) is on the line.
B) It is parallel to the line $y=5x$.
C) It is parallel to the x-axis.
D) It has a slope of 5.

38

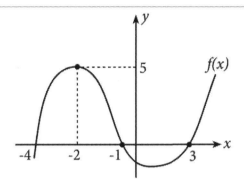

For which value(s) of x is $f(x)$ equal to zero?

A) 0
B) -2
C) -4, -1
D) -4, -1, 3

39

Melisa is a repair technician for a computer company. Each week, she receives a batch of notebooks that need repairs. The number of notebooks that she has left to fix at the end of each day can be estimated with the equation $L = 124-21d$, where is the number of notebooks left and is the number of days she has worked that week.

What is the meaning of the value 124 in this equation?

A) Melisa will complete the repairs within 124 days.
B) Melisa starts each week with 124 notebooks to fix.
C) Melisa repairs notebooks at a rate of 124 per hour.
D) Melisa repairs notebooks at a rate of 124 per day.

CONTINUE ▶

40

Let $f(x) = x^2 - 3$

If $g(f(x)) = \sqrt{x^2 + 4}$, which of the following describes $g(x)$?

A) $g(x) = \sqrt{x+1}$
B) $g(x) = \sqrt{x+7}$
C) $g(x) = \sqrt{x^2 + 7}$
D) $g(x) = \sqrt{x^2 - 7}$

41

On Saturday afternoon, Arman send m text messages each hour for 4 hours, and Rona sent p text messages each hour for 5 hours. Which of the following represents the total number of messages sent by Arman and Rona on Saturday afternoon?

A) $9mp$
B) $20mp$
C) $4m + 5p$
D) $9mp$

42

The function f has the property for all values of $f(x) = x$. Which of the following statements about the graph of $f(x)$ is true?

A) It is a line with slope 0.
B) It is a line with slope 1.
C) It is a line with slope -1.
D) Its slope is undefined.

43

If the points (6,-5) and (8,7) are on the line k, which of the following points are not on the line?

A) (5,-11)
B) (7,1)
C) (10,19)
D) (-4, 18)

44

$$3x + 5y = 9$$
$$2y - x = 8$$

What is the solution (x,y) to the system of equations above?

A) (2,-3)
B) (-2,3)
C) (0.5,1.5)
D) (6,4)

45

The function $f(x)$ has the property such that $f(x) = a$ for all values of x.

Which of the following statements about the graph of $f(x)$ is true?

A) It is a horizontal line.
B) It is a line with slope 1.
C) It is a line with slope -1.
D) It is a vertical line.

CONTINUE ▶

46

x	0	1	2	3
$f(x)$	-7	-6	-3	2

The table above gives values of the quadratic function $f(x)$ for selected values of x. What is the value of $f(4)$?

A) -3

B) 9

C) 10

D) 23

47

$$y = 4x + b$$

If the midpoint of A(3,2) and B(-1,4) is on the line given above, what is the value of b?

A) 1

B) -1

C) -5

D) -9

48

Half-life is the time required for a quantity to reduce to half its initial value. The term is commonly used in nuclear physics to describe how quickly unstable atoms undergo, or how long stable atoms survive radioactive decay.

The half-life of a medication prescribed by a doctor is 8 hours. How many mg of this medication is left after 24 hours if the doctor prescribed 400 mg?

A) 12.5

B) 25

C) 50

D) 100

49

$$\frac{4y^2 - 100}{y + 5} = 12$$

What is the value of y ?

A) -2

B) 8

C) 12

D) 17

CONTINUE ▶

50

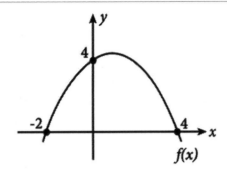

f(x)

The parabola of f(x) is given above. Find the maximum value of f(x) ?

A) 4.5

B) 5

C) 5.5

D) 6

51

What is the value of $f(7)$ if $f(x)$ is a linear function, $f(2) = 13$, and $f(5) = 22$?

A) 25

B) 28

C) 31

D) 33

52

Which of the following best describes the graph of the equation $2x = 3y - 1$ in the xy plane?

A) The line has a positive x-intercept and negative y-intercept.

B) The line has a negative x-intercept and positive y-intercept.

C) The line has a positive slope and negative y-intercept.

D) The line has a negative slope and positive y-intercept.

53

x	$f(x)$
-1	-5
0	-3
1	-1
2	1

x	$g(x)$
0	4
1	-1
2	-2
3	-5

Some values of the functions $f(x)$ and $g(x)$ are given above. What is the value of $f(g(1))$?

A) -5

B) -3

C) -1

D) 1

CONTINUE ▶

54

$$f(\text{ABC}) = \text{ABC} + \text{AB} + \text{A}$$

In the function given above A, B, and C lie from 1 to 9, ABC is a three digit number, AB is a two digit number.

What is the value of $f(321) + f(653)$?

A) 356

B) 724

C) 1,080

D) 1,180

55

$$\frac{6x+20}{x+2} = A + \frac{B}{x+2}$$

Based on the expression above, find A+B?

A) 14

B) 20

C) 26

D) 28

56

$$a+3 = b+4$$

$$\frac{1}{a+3} + \frac{1}{b+4} = 1$$

Based on the equations above, what is the value of $a + b$?

A) -1

B) -2

C) -3

D) -4

57

$$\frac{m-1}{m-3} = \frac{m-5}{m-4}$$

According to the equation above what is the value of m?

A) $\frac{8}{5}$

B) $\frac{13}{4}$

C) $\frac{9}{4}$

D) $\frac{11}{3}$

CONTINUE ▶

58

$$\frac{5x}{x-3}+\frac{2x}{2x-6}=\frac{54}{3x-9}$$

What value of x satisfies the equation given above?

A) 3

B) 6

C) There is no solution.

D) There are infinitely many solutions.

59

Let $x=\dfrac{a+1}{a-3}$, what is $x-1$ in terms of a?

A) $\dfrac{2a-2}{a-3}$

B) $\dfrac{4}{a-3}$

C) $\dfrac{a}{a-3}$

D) $\dfrac{a+1}{a-4}$

60

$$\frac{1+\dfrac{1}{x}}{\dfrac{1}{x^2}-1}$$

What is the simplified form of the equation above?

A) $\dfrac{1}{x-1}$

B) $\dfrac{1}{1-x}$

C) $\dfrac{-x}{x-1}$

D) $\dfrac{x-1}{x}$

61

$$\frac{5(k+2)-4}{6}=\frac{8-(3-k)}{3}$$

What is the value of k in the equation above?

A) $\dfrac{12}{21}$

B) $\dfrac{4}{3}$

C) $\dfrac{3}{2}$

D) $\dfrac{16}{3}$

62

If $3^x + 3^{x+1} + 3^{x+2} = 39$, then what is 2^x?

A) 1
B) 2
C) 4
D) 8

63

$$\frac{4^x}{2^x + 2^x} = 32$$

What is the value of x which satisfies the equation given above?

A) 2
B) 4
C) 6
D) 8

64

$$2^{20} + 16^5 + 4^{10} + 32^4 + 2^{20}$$

What is the sum of the expression above?

A) 2^{20}
B) 2^{22}
C) $5 \cdot 2^{20}$
D) $5 \cdot 2^{100}$

65

If $a^3 = b^9 c^{12}$ and a, b and c are positive numbers, then what is the value of a?

A) $\dfrac{b^9 c^{12}}{3}$
B) $b^3 c^4$
C) $b^{27} c^{36}$
D) $b^6 c^9$

66

$$\sqrt[4]{4^8 + \frac{4^8 - 4^{10}}{2^4}}$$

What is the result of the operation given above?

A) 4
B) 8
C) 16
D) 32

67

$$\sqrt{\frac{4^7 + 4^7 + 4^7 + 4^7}{2^6 + 2^6 + 2^6 + 2^6}} = A$$

According to the equation above what is the value of A?

A) 2
B) 4
C) 16
D) 64

68

$$a = \sqrt{2}$$
$$b = \sqrt{7}$$
$$c = \sqrt{56}$$

What is the value of $\dfrac{c}{a^3 b}$?

A) 1
B) 2
C) 7
D) $\sqrt{2}$

71

$$\frac{\sqrt{108} + \sqrt{12}}{\sqrt{48}}$$

What is the result of the operation above?

A) $\sqrt{3}$
B) $3\sqrt{3}$
C) $2\sqrt{3}$
D) 2

69

$$x - \sqrt{2x} = 4$$

Based on the equation above, what is the value of x?

A) 6
B) 8
C) 9
D) 12

72

$$a + b = 4$$
$$b - c = 3$$

What is the value of $ab - ac + b^2 - bc$?

A) 4
B) 8
C) 12
D) 16

70

$$\sqrt[x]{a} \cdot \sqrt[y]{a}$$

What is the equivalent of the expression above?

A) $\sqrt[xy]{a}$
B) $\sqrt[xy]{a^2}$
C) $\sqrt[x+y]{a^{xy}}$
D) $\sqrt[xy]{a^{x+y}}$

73

$$\frac{(x-2)^2(x+2)}{(x-2)}$$

Which of the following is equivalent to the expression above?

A) $-(x-2)^2$
B) $x^2 - 2x - 4$
C) $x^2 + 2x + 4$
D) $x^2 - 4$

CONTINUE ▶

74

$$(3a^2 - ab - 2) - (4a^2 - ab + 5)$$

Which of the following is equivalent to the expression above?

A) $-a^2 - 7$
B) $-a^2 + 3$
C) $7a^2 - 2ab + 3$
D) $-a^2 - 2ab + 3$

75

If $a = 3x^2 - x + 2$, $b = x^2 + 5$, $c = 4x - 7$, then find $2a - (3b + c)$?

A) $2x^2 - 5x - 10$
B) $3x^2 + 2x - 18$
C) $3x^2 - 6x - 4$
D) $9x^2 + 2x + 12$

76

If $x^2 + mx + n = (x - 2)(x + 6)$, what is the value of mn?

A) -48
B) -12
C) 4
D) 24

77

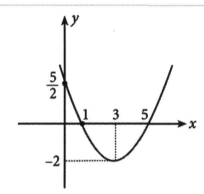

Which of the following represents the parabola shown above?

A) $f(x) = \dfrac{1}{2}(x - 3)^2 - 2$

B) $f(x) = \dfrac{1}{2}(x + 3)^2 + \dfrac{5}{2}$

C) $f(x) = (x - 3)^2 + \dfrac{5}{2}$

D) $f(x) = (x + 2)^2 + 3$

78

$$y = -4x^2 + 16x$$

How many solutions does the quadratic equation given above have?

A) There is only one solution.
B) There are two solutions.
C) There is no solution.
D) It can not be determined.

79

If $P(x) = ax^2 + bx + c$ and $P(1) = 8$, $P(-1) = 6$, then find the value of $a + c$.

A) 7
B) 10
C) 14
D) 48

80

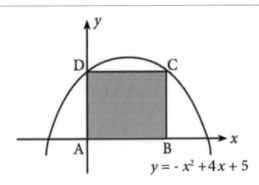

$$y = -x^2 + 4x + 5$$

Given the graph and formula of the parabola above, what is the area of the rectangle ABCD?

A) 16
B) 20
C) 25
D) 36

SECTION 2 - ALGEBRA

#	Answer	Topic	Subtopic	#	Answer	Topic	Subtopic	#	Answer	Topic	Subtopic	#	Answer	Topic	Subtopic
1	D	TB	SB14	21	B	TB	SB1	41	C	TA	SA3	61	B	TB	SB7
2	B	TC	SC5	22	A	TB	SB14	42	B	TA	SA5	62	B	TB	SB5
3	C	TB	SB14	23	A	TA	SA9	43	D	TA	SA5	63	C	TB	SB5
4	A	TA	SA9	24	D	TC	SC5	44	B	TA	SA9	64	C	TB	SB5
5	B	TA	SA5	25	D	TB	SB8	45	A	TB	SB14	65	B	TB	SB5
6	B	TC	SC5	26	A	TA	SA1	46	B	TB	SB14	66	B	TB	SB6
7	B	TB	SB11	27	C	TC	SC1	47	B	TA	SA5	67	C	TB	SB6
8	B	TB	SB8	28	B	TC	SC5	48	C	TA	SA3	68	A	TB	SB6
9	C	TA	SA5	29	A	TB	SB14	49	B	TB	SB7	69	B	TB	SB6
10	B	TB	SB13	30	A	TB	SB8	50	A	TB	SB1	70	D	TB	SB6
11	A	TB	SB2	31	D	TA	SA5	51	B	TB	SB14	71	D	TB	SB6
12	D	TA	SA5	32	C	TB	SB14	52	B	TA	SA5	72	C	TB	SB8
13	D	TA	SA1	33	C	TB	SB1	53	A	TB	SB14	73	D	TB	SB8
14	D	TB	SB2	34	D	TB	SB12	54	C	TB	SB14	74	A	TB	SB8
15	D	TA	SA5	35	A	TA	SA3	55	A	TB	SB7	75	C	TB	SB8
16	D	TB	SB14	36	A	TB	SB14	56	C	TB	SB7	76	A	TB	SB8
17	D	TA	SA1	37	A	TA	SA5	57	D	TB	SB7	77	A	TB	SB1
18	A	TB	SB11	38	D	TB	SB14	58	C	TB	SB7	78	B	TB	SB1
19	B	TB	SB13	39	B	TA	SA3	59	B	TB	SB7	79	A	TB	SB1
20	B	TB	SB2	40	B	TB	SB14	60	C	TB	SB7	80	B	TB	SB1

Topics & Subtopics

Code	Description	Code	Description
SA1	Solving Linear Equations & Inequalities	SB5	Exponents & Rational Exponents
SA3	Linear Equations & Inequalities Word Problems	SB6	Radicals & Radical Equations
SA5	Graphing Linear Equations	SB7	Operations with Rational Expressions
SA9	Systems of Equations	SB8	Operations with Polynomials
SB1	Quadratic Equations	SC1	Ratios, Rates & Proportions
SB11	Linear & Quadratic Systems	SC5	Scatterplots
SB12	Structure in Expressions	TA	Heart of Algebra
SB13	Isolating Quantities	TB	Passport to Advanced Mathematics
SB14	Functions	TC	Problem Solving and Data Analysis
SB2	Nonlinear Graphs & Expressions		

CONTINUE ▶

1

$$f(x) = \sqrt{x^2 + 16}$$

Which of the following is the domain of the function given above?

A) All real numbers greater than -16.

B) All real numbers greater than -4.

C) All real numbers greater than 4.

D) All real numbers.

Inside the square root should be zero. Because there is an x^2 term then domain is all reall numbers

2

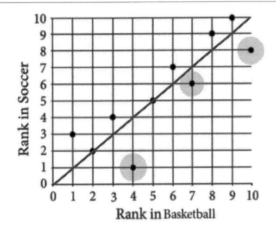

The ranking of 10 students in two sports is shown above in the scatter plot. How many students received a better rank in Soccer than Basketball?

A) 2

B) 3

C) 4

D) 5

Below the line of y=x, there are 3 points for which students have a better rank in soccer

Soccer 1, Basketball 4
Soccer 6, Basketball 7
Soccer 6, Basketball 10

3

$$K@L = 3K - 2L$$

M @ N = 3M - 2N

According to the operation defined above, what is the value of (M@N) @P?

(3M - 2N)@ P = 3(3M - 2N) - 2P = 9M - 6N - 2P

A) 3M - 2N +3P

B) 3M - 2N - 2P

C) 9M - 6N - 2P

D) 3M + 3N - 2P

4

$$-6 < x < 4$$
-5

$$-2 < y < 11$$
10

If both x and y are integers, what is the minimum integer value of 3x - 5y?

To minimize 3x-5y you should select minimum integer value for x and maximum integer value for y

A) -65

B) -73

C) -74

D) -76

3·(-5) - 5·(10)
-15 - 50 = -65

CONTINUE ▶

5

$$3x = \frac{1}{4}y - 2$$

+2   *×2*

In the *xy*-plane, which of the following best describes the graph of the equation given above?

positive slope

$$4 \cdot \frac{1}{4}y = (3x+2) \cdot 4 \qquad y = 12x + 8$$

positive

A) It has a negative x-intercept and *y-intercept* positive slope.

B) It has positive y-intercept and postive slope.

C) It has positive x-intercept and positive y -intercept.

D) It has a negative slope and postive a negative y-intercept.

6

Hena wants to make a scatter plot comparing the life expectancy, represented in the *y*-axis, and the air pollution, given in the *x*-axis.

Which line fits best for Hena's expectation about her scatter plot?

A) A vertical line

B) A negative slope line

C) A positive slope line

D) A horizontal line

A negative correlation is expected between the life expectancy and air pollution

7

$$y = x^2 - 24$$
$$y = x - 12$$

Which ordered pair is a solution of the system of equations given above?

$$x^2 - 24 = x - 12$$
−x+12   *−x +12*

A) (4,8)

$$x^2 - x - 12 = 0$$

B) (4,−8)

$$(x-4)(x+3) = 0$$

C) (2,−10)

D) (12,0)

$$x - 4 = 0 \qquad x + 3 = 0$$
+4 +4   *−3 −3*
$$x = 4 \qquad\qquad x = 3$$
$$y = x - 12 \qquad y = x - 12$$
$$y = 4 - 12 \qquad y = 3 - 12$$
$$y = -8 \qquad\qquad y = -9$$
$$(4, -8) \qquad\qquad (3, -9)$$

8

$$(-x^2 + 3x + 7)(6x^5 - 3x^4 + x^2 + 2x - 5)$$

After the multiplication of the polynomials given above, what will be the coefficent of the term x^3?

You don't need to multiply everything. Just multiply the terms that gives x^3.

A) -2

B) 1

C) 3

D) 5

$$-x^2 \cdot 2x \qquad +3x \cdot x^2$$
$$-2x^3 + 3x^3 = \boxed{1}x^3$$

$$E = mc^2$$

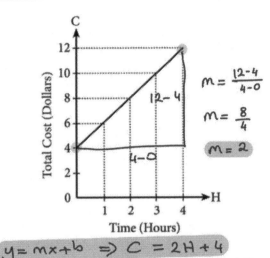

$m = \dfrac{12-4}{4-0}$

$m = \dfrac{8}{4}$

$m = 2$

$y = mx + b \Rightarrow C = 2H + 4$

The graph above displays the total cost (C) in dollars of renting a toy car for (H) hours. Which of the following is true?

A) C - intercept is the hourly price of renting.

B) The slope of the graph is the initial price of renting.

C) C = 4 + 2H is the relationship between C and H

D) Hourly price for renting is $4

In physics, mass–energy equivalence is a concept formulated by Albert Einstein that explains the relationship between mass and energy. Which of the following expresses speed of light c in terms of mass and energy ?

A) $c = \dfrac{E}{m}$

B) $c = \sqrt{\dfrac{E}{m}}$

C) $c = \sqrt{E - m}$

D) $c = \dfrac{E}{2m}$

$\dfrac{E}{m} = \dfrac{m c^2}{m}$

$\sqrt{c^2} = \sqrt{\dfrac{E}{m}}$

$c = \sqrt{\dfrac{E}{m}}$

11

q	N(q)
0	1400
1	2800
2	5600
3	11200
4	22400

The relationship netween $N(q)$ and q is defined in the chart above. Which of the following equations best describes this relationship?

A) $N(q) = 1400 \times (2)^q$

B) $N(q) = 1400 \times 2q$

C) $N(q) = 1400 \times 2q^2$

D) $N(q) = 1400 \times q^2$

N is becoming 2 times bigger when q is increased by 1. N is proportianel with 2^q

12

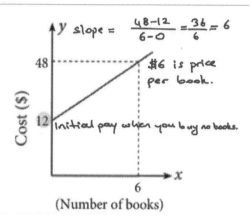

slope $= \dfrac{48-12}{6-0} = \dfrac{36}{6} = 6$

$6 is price per book.

Initial pay when you buy no books.

(Number of books)

The graph above shows the cost of the books in a book fair. Which of the following statements is NOT correct?

A) You should pay an entrance fee even if you don't buy any book.

B) The slope of the line gives the price of one book.

C) Entrance fee for the book fair is $12.

D) If you buy 3 books you will pay $24.

To by 3 books, you should pay 12 + 3·6 = $30

13

$$4m - 4 \le 0$$

Based on the inequality given above, what is the greatest possible value of $5m + 2$?

A) 2 $4m - 4 \le 0$ $\frac{4m}{4} \le \frac{4}{4}$ $m \le 1$
         $+4$ $+4$

B) 3

C) 5 $5m + 2 = 5 \cdot 1 + 2 = 7$

D) 7

14

In 2012, the number of cell phone subscribers in the small town of Molnar were 1,500. The number of subscribers increased by 60% per year after 2012. How many cell phone subscribers were in Molnar in 2015?

After 60% increase number of subscribers will be 160% of the previous year.

A) 1,800
                  2012   2013   2014
B) 2,400   1,500   1,500·($\frac{160}{100}$)   1,500·($\frac{160}{100}$)·($\frac{160}{100}$)

C) 3,840
                  2015
D) 6,144   1,500·($\frac{160}{100}$)·($\frac{160}{100}$)·($\frac{160}{100}$) = 6144

15

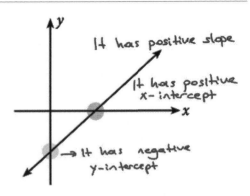
It has positive slope
It has positive x-intercept
It has negative y-intercept

Which of the following statements about the line is true? $3x - 4y + 10 = 0$ has positive x-intercept, negative y-intercept, and positive slope. So it can be the line equation.

A) The slope of the line is negative.

B) y-intercept of the line is positive.

C) x-intercept of the line is negative.

D) $3x - 4y + 10 = 0$ can be the line equation.

16

$$f(x) = \frac{3}{4}x - 12$$

For the function given above, what domain value corresponds to the range value of 24?

A) 6   Range is the value of y
          Domain is the value of x
B) 27
          $24 = \frac{3}{4}x - 12$
C) 36 $+12$ $+12$

D) 48 $\frac{4}{3} \cdot 36 = \frac{3}{4}x \cdot \frac{4}{3} \Rightarrow x = 48$

17

$$0 < 1 - \frac{2a}{5} \leq \frac{3}{5}$$

Which value below is NOT possible for a?

A) 1
B) 1.5
C) 2
D) 2.5

handwritten work:
$5 \cdot 0 < \left(1 - \frac{2a}{5}\right) \cdot 5 \leq \frac{3}{5} \cdot 5$
$0 < 5 - 2a \leq 3$
$-5 \quad -5 \quad -5$
$-5 < -2a \leq -2$
$\frac{-5}{-2} \quad \frac{-2a}{-2} \quad \frac{-2}{-2}$
$\frac{5}{2} > a \geq 1$
a can not take the value of 2.5

18

$$y = 2x^2 + 1$$
$$y = 2x + 5$$

What values of x satisfy the system of equations given above?

A) -1 and 2
B) -1 and 3
C) 2 and 1
D) 0 and 2

handwritten work:
$2x^2 + 1 = 2x + 5$
$-2x -5 \quad -2x -5$
$2x^2 - 2x - 4 = 0$
$\frac{2x^2}{2} - \frac{2x}{2} - \frac{4}{2}$
$x^2 - x - 2 = 0$
$(x-2)(x+1) = 0$
$x - 2 = 0 \quad x+1 = 0$
$+2 +2 \quad -1$
$x = 2 \quad x = -1$

19

$$PV = nRT$$

Ideal gas law is given above. How can you express temperature, T, in terms of other variables?

A) $PVnR$
B) $\dfrac{PV}{nR}$
C) $PV + nR$
D) $PV - nR$

handwritten work:
$\dfrac{PV}{nR} = \dfrac{nRT}{nR}$
$T = \dfrac{PV}{nR}$

20

$$P(t) = P_0\left(1 + \frac{r}{100}\right)^n$$

The formula given above models the population of a city n years after an initial population of P_0 people is counted. The population grows at a constant rate of $r\%$ per year. The population of the city was 860,000 in 2010. Assume the population grows at a constant rate of 4% per year. According to this formula, which of the following is an expression for the population of the city in the year 2020?

A) $860,000(4)^{10}$
B) $860,000(1.04)^{10}$
C) $(860,000 \times 0.6)^{10}$
D) $(860,000 \times 1.04)^{10}$

handwritten work:
$P(t) = 860,000\left(1 + \frac{4}{100}\right)^n$
$n = 2020 - 2010 = 10$
$P(t) = 860,000 (1.04)^{10}$

CONTINUE ▶

21

$$3x^2 + y^2 = 76$$

Based on the equation given above, which of the following is a possible value for y if both x and y are integers?

$$3x^2 + y^2 = 76$$

A) -5 $3x^2 + (-5)^2 = 76$ $3x^2 + 0^2 = 76$
         No integer value for x   No integer value for x

B) -1 $3x^2 + (-1)^2 = 76$ $3x^2 + 5^2 = 76$
         $3x^2 + 1 = 76$ No integer value for x

C) 0 $\frac{3x^2}{3} = \frac{75}{3}$
         -1 -1

D) 5 $x^2 = 25$ $x = 5$

-1 is a possible value for y

22

$$f(x) = \frac{23}{x+2}$$

What is the range of $f(x)$ if it is defined on all real numbers except -2?

A) All real numbers

B) All real numbers except -3

C) All real numbers except -2   (Domain)

D) All real numbers greater than -2

Range is all real numbers. It can be positive or negative, but all numbers.

23

$$\bar{a} < 0 < \overset{+}{b} < \overset{+}{c}$$

Based on the given expression;

I. $\bar{a} + \overset{+}{c} > 0$ may be true, not always!

II. $a^2 < b^2$ may be true, not always!

III. $ab > ac$ c is bigger than a, but after multiplying with a negative number, a, it will be smaller.

which of the inequalities are always true?

A) Only III

B) Only II

C) I and III

D) II and III

24

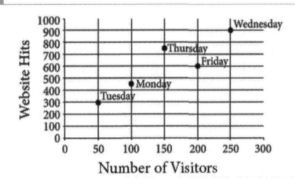

The graph given above shows the number of visitors and website hits. On which day is the ratio of website hits to the number of visitors the smallest?

A) Monday : $\frac{450}{100} = 4.5$

B) Tuesday : $\frac{300}{50} = 6$

C) Wednesday: $\frac{900}{250} = 3.6$

D) Friday   : $\frac{600}{200} = 3$ smallest ratio

25

$$(2a^2 - 3ab - 1) - (3a^2 - 5ab - 4)$$

Which of the following is equivalent to the expression above?

A) $-a^2 + 2ab - 5$

B) $-a^2 - 8ab - 5$ $(2a^2 - 3ab - 1) - (3a^2 - 5ab - 4)$

C) $5a^2 - 8ab - 5$ $2a^2 - 3ab - 1 - 3a^2 + 5ab + 4$

D) $-a^2 + 2ab + 3$ $-a^2 + 2ab + 3$

26

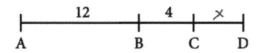

In the figure above AB=12, BC=4 and AD=3CD. What is the value of $\dfrac{BD}{BC}$?

A) 3 $AD = 3CD$ $\dfrac{BD}{BC} = \dfrac{4+8}{4} = 3$

$12 + 4 + x = 3x$

B) 4 $-x \quad -x$

C) 6 $\dfrac{16}{2} = \dfrac{2x}{2}$

D) 8 $x = 8$

27

In a Research Center in Massachusetts, biologists are working on a project about DNA sequencing. In DNA sequencing, it costs approximately 20 cents to sequence 500 base pairs.

If a researcher would like to sequence a gene consisting of 60,000 base pairs, how much would it cost to obtain the sequence?

A) $12 $\dfrac{60{,}000}{500} \times 0.2 = 120 \times 0.2 = \$24$

B) $16

C) $24

D) $48

28

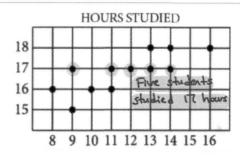

The scatter plot given above shows the number of hours, between 15 and 18, studied by 12 students of various ages, between 8 and 16, at after-school study program.

Which of the following is NOT true, according to this scatter plot?

A) More than half of the students studied more than 16 hours.

B) Four students studied exactly 17 hours.

C) One 12 years old student studied 17 hours.

D) Most of the students were over 9 years old.

29

$$f(x) = \sqrt{x+3} \quad \text{for all values } x \geq 0$$
$$f(x) = x^2 + 5 \quad \text{for all values of } x < 0$$

Given the function above, what is the value of $f(-4) - f(13)$?

A) 17

B) 21

C) 25

D) 173

(handwritten work):
$\left((-4)^2 + 5\right) - \left(\sqrt{13+3}\right)$
$16 + 5 - \sqrt{16}$
$21 - 4 = 17$

30

$$P(x) = 7x^4 - 3x^3 + 5x + 3$$
$$Q(x) = -4x^4 - 2x^3 - x^2 - 3x + 4$$

Polynomials $P(x)$ **and** $Q(x)$ **are given above. Find the polynomial** $2P(x) - 3Q(x)$.

A) $26x^4 + 3x^2 + 19x - 6$

B) $26x^4 + 3x^2 + 13x + 18$

C) $13x^4 - 4x^3 - 2x^2 - 6x + 17$

D) $2x^4 - 12x^3 - 3x^2 + x - 6$

(handwritten work):
$2\left(7x^4 - 3x^3 + 5x + 3\right) - 3\left(-4x^4 - 2x^3 - x^2 - 3x + 4\right)$
$14x^4 - 6x^3 + 10x + 6 + 12x^4 + 6x^3 + 3x^2 + 9x - 12$
$26x^4 + 3x^2 + 19x - 6$

31

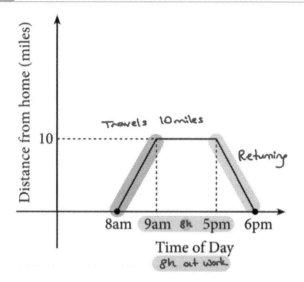

Travels 10 miles

Returning

8h

8h at work

The graph above shows the distance of Sam from his home during the particular hours of a day.

Which of the expressions below can NOT be a correct information based on this graph?

A) Sam returns back to his home at 6pm.
B) Sam's Office is 10 miles away from his house.
C) Sam went to the hospital, stayed there 8 hours.
D) Between 8am and 6pm Sam stayed at home.

32

$$A = \{@, \#, \&\}$$

$$B = \{@, \#, !\}$$

Which of the following is a function defined from A to B?

Domain value cannot have more than one range value.

A) $\{ (@, @), (@, \#), (@, !) \}$
B) $\{ (@, @), (\#, \#), (!, !) \}$! is not member of A
C) $\{ (@, @), (\#, \#), (\&, @) \}$
D) $\{ (@, @), (\#, !), (@, \&) \}$

33

$$y = (m-3)x^2 - mx + 11$$

If the vertex of the parabola is on (2,7), what is the value of *m*?

$$\text{Vertex} = \left(-\frac{b}{2a}, f\left(-\frac{b}{2a}\right)\right)$$

A) 2

B) 3 $-\frac{b}{2a} = 2$ $\frac{-(-m)}{2(m-3)} = 2$

C) 4

D) 6 $\frac{m}{2m-6} = \frac{2}{1}$ $m = 4m - 12$

$+12 \rightarrow m$ $-m + 12$

$\frac{12}{3} = \frac{3m}{3}$

$m = 4$

34

If you add 3 to the numerator of $\dfrac{a}{b}$, how much

the value of $\dfrac{a}{b}$ increases?

A) 3 $\dfrac{a}{b} \rightarrow \dfrac{a+3}{b} = \dfrac{a}{b} + \dfrac{3}{b}$

B) 3*a*

C) $\dfrac{3}{a}$

D) $\dfrac{3}{b}$

35

$$P = 240 - 15d$$

Adam wants to sell all the products in his store. The number of products in the store as a function of *d* is estimated with the equation given above. In the equation *P* is the number of products left in the store and *d* is the number of days the store is open.

What is the meaning of the value 15 in this equation?   *Number of products are decreasing by 15 everyday*

A) The number of products that are sold per day

B) The number of days to sell all the products in the store

C) The rate of increase of products per day

D) The number of products left in the store at the end of each day

36

$$A \& B = \frac{A}{B} + A \cdot B$$

If A = 8 and B = -2, what is the value of A&B?

A) -20 $8 \& -2 = \dfrac{8}{-2} + 8 \cdot (-2)$

B) -12

C) 16 $= -4 - 16$

D) 20 $= -20$

37

Which of the following for is true for a line in the xy-plane that has the equation $x=5$?

A) The point $(5,-1)$ is on the line.
B) It is parallel to the line $y=5x$.
C) It is parallel to the x-axis.
D) It has a slope of 5.

It is parallel to y-axis
It has no slope.
(5,-1) is on the line.

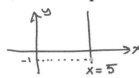

$x=5$

38

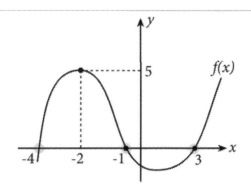

$f(x)$

-4 -2 -1 3

For which value(s) of x is $f(x)$ equal to zero?

A) 0   The points at which the graph touches x-axis are the roots of the function.
B) -2
C) -4, -1
D) -4, -1, 3

39

Melisa is a repair technician for a computer company. Each week, she receives a batch of notebooks that need repairs. The number of notebooks that she has left to fix at the end of each day can be estimated with the equation $L = 124-21d$, where is the number of notebooks left and is the number of days she has worked that week.

What is the meaning of the value 124 in this equation?

At day 0 melisa has 124 notebooks. 124 is the number of notebooks

A) Melisa will complete the repairs within 124 days.
B) Melisa starts each week with 124 notebooks to fix.
C) Melisa repairs notebooks at a rate of 124 per hour.
D) Melisa repairs notebooks at a rate of 124 per day.

40

Let $f(x)=x^2-3$

If $g(f(x))=\sqrt{x^2+4}$, which of the following describes $g(x)$?

A) $g(x)=\sqrt{x+1}$ $\sqrt{f(x)+7}=\sqrt{x^2-3+7}$
B) $g(x)=\sqrt{x+7}$
C) $g(x)=\sqrt{x^2+7}$ $g(x)=\sqrt{x+4}$
D) $g(x)=\sqrt{x^2-7}$

41

On Saturday afternoon, Arman send *m* text messages each hour for 4 hours, and Rona sent *p* text messages each hour for 5 hours. Which of the following represents the total number of messages sent by Arman and Rona on Saturday afternoon?

A) $9mp$

B) $20mp$

C) $4m+5p$

D) $9mp$

Arman : $4 \cdot m$

Rona : $5 \cdot p$

$4m + 5p$

42

The function *f* has the property for all values of $f(x) = x$. Which of the following statements about the graph of $f(x)$ is true?

A) It is a line with slope 0.

B) It is a line with slope 1.

C) It is a line with slope -1.　The slope of

D) Its slope is undefined.　the line is 1.

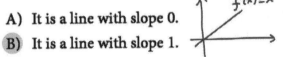

43

If the points (6,-5) and (8,7) are on the line *k*, which of the following points are not on the line?

A) (5,-11)

B) (7,1)

C) (10,19)

D) (-4, 18)

$(8,7)$　$slope = \dfrac{7 - (-5)}{8 - 6}$

$(6,-5)$　Δy

$slope = \dfrac{12}{2} = 6$

$(5,-11)$ $(8,7)$　$m = \dfrac{7 - (-11)}{8-5} = 6$

$(7,1)$ $(8,7)$　$m = \dfrac{7-1}{8-7} = 6$

$(10,19)$ $(8,7)$　$m = \dfrac{7-19}{8-10} = 6$

$(-4,18)$　$(8,7)$　$m = \dfrac{7-18}{8-(-4)} \ne 6$

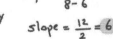

44

$$3x + 5y = 9$$
$$2y - x = 8$$

What is the solution (x,y) to the system of equations above?

A) (2,-3)

B) (-2,3)

C) (0.5,1.5)

D) (6,4)

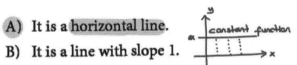

$3x + 5y = 9 \Rightarrow 3x + 5y = 9$
$-x + 2y = 8 \Rightarrow -3x + 6y = 24$

$\dfrac{11y}{11} = \dfrac{33}{11}$

$y = 3$

$3x + 5y = 9$
$3x + 5 \cdot 3 = 9$
$3x + 15 = 9$
$-15 \quad -15$
$\dfrac{3x}{3} = \dfrac{-6}{3}$　$x = -2$

45

The function $f(x)$ has the property such that $f(x) = a$ for all values of *x*.

Which of the following statements about the graph of $f(x)$ is true?

A) It is a horizontal line.

B) It is a line with slope 1.

C) It is a line with slope -1.

D) It is a vertical line.

constant function

CONTINUE ▶

46

x	0	1	2	3
$f(x)$	-7	-6	-3	2

$$y = ax^2 + bx + c$$

The table above gives values of the quadratic function $f(x)$ for selected values of x. What is the value of $f(4)$?

A) -3

B) 9

C) 10

D) 23

$a \cdot 0^2 + b \cdot 0 + c = -7$ $c = -7$

$a \cdot 1^2 + b \cdot 1 - 7 = -6$ $a + b = 1$

$a \cdot 2^2 + b \cdot 2 - 7 = -3$ $4a + 2b = 4$

$\begin{array}{r} -2a - 2b = -2 \\ + 4a + 2b = 4 \\ \hline 2a = 2 \end{array}$ $\begin{array}{l} a+b=1 \\ 1+b=1 \\ b=0 \end{array}$

$\frac{2a}{2} = \frac{2}{2}$

$a = 1$ $f(x) = x^2 - 7$

$f(4) = 4^2 - 7 = 9$

47

$$y = 4x + b$$

If the midpoint of A(3,2) and B(-1,4) is on the line given above, what is the value of b?

A) 1

B) -1

C) -5

D) -9

Midpoint $\left(\frac{3+(-1)}{2}, \frac{2+4}{2}\right)$ Midpoint $(1,3)$

$y = 4x + b$

$3 = 4 \cdot 1 + b$

$3 = 4 + b$

$-4 \quad -4$

$b = -1$

48

Half-life is the time required for a quantity to reduce to half its initial value. The term is commonly used in nuclear physics to describe how quickly unstable atoms undergo, or how long stable atoms survive radioactive decay.

The half-life of a medication prescribed by a doctor is 8 hours. How many mg of this medication is left after 24 hours if the doctor prescribed 400 mg?

A) 12.5

B) 25

C) 50

D) 100

$8h + 8h + 8h = 24h$

400mg → 200mg → 100mg → 50mg

49

$$\frac{4y^2 - 100}{y + 5} = 12$$

What is the value of y ?

A) -2

B) 8

C) 12

D) 17

$\frac{4y^2 - 100}{y+5} = 12$ $\frac{4(y^2-25)}{(y+5)} = 12$

$\frac{4(y+5)(y-5)}{(y+5)} = 12$ $\frac{4(y-5)}{4} = \frac{12}{4}$

$y - 5 = 3$

$+5 \quad +5$

$y = 8$

CONTINUE ▶

50

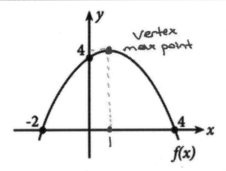

The parabola of $f(x)$ is given above. Find the maximum value of $f(x)$?

A) 4.5 $f(x) = a(x+2)(x-4)$

B) 5 $f(0) = a \cdot (0+2) \cdot (0-4) = -8a = 4$

C) 5.5 $f(x) = -\frac{1}{2}(x+2)(x-4)$ $a = -\frac{1}{2}$

D) 6 $f(1) = -\frac{1}{2}(1+2)(1-4) = -\frac{1}{2} \cdot 3 \cdot -3 = 4.5$

51

What is the value of $f(7)$ if $f(x)$ is a linear function, $f(2) = 13$, and $f(5) = 22$?

$f(x) = ax+b$

A) 25 $f(2) = 2a+b = 13$ $2a+b=13$

B) 28 $f(5) = 5a+b = 22$ $2 \cdot 3 + b = 13$

C) 31 $\frac{-3a}{3} = \frac{-9}{-3}$ $6+b = 13$

D) 33 $a = 3$ $b = 7$

$f(7) = 7 \cdot 3 + 7 = 21 + 7 = 28$

52

Which of the following best describes the graph of the equation $2x = 3y - 1$ in the xy plane? $2x = 3y - 1$ $3y = 2x + 1$

$y = \frac{2}{3}x + \frac{1}{3}$

A) The line has a positive x-intercept and negative y-intercept. $0 = \frac{2}{3}x + \frac{1}{3}$

B) The line has a negative x-intercept and positive y-intercept. $y = \frac{2}{3} \cdot 0 + \frac{1}{3}$

C) The line has a positive slope and negative y-intercept.

D) The line has a negative slope and positive y-intercept.

53

x	$f(x)$
-1	-5
0	-3
1	-1
2	1

x	$g(x)$
0	4
1	-1
2	-2
3	-5

$g(1) = -1$

Some values of the functions $f(x)$ and $g(x)$ are given above. What is the value of $f(g(1))$?

A) -5 $f(g(1)) = f(-1) = -5$

B) -3

C) -1

D) 1

54

$$f(ABC) = ABC + AB + A$$

In the function given above A, B, and C lie from 1 to 9, ABC is a three digit number, AB is a two digit number.

What is the value of $f(321) + f(653)$?

A) 356

B) 724

C) 1,080

D) 1,180

$f(321) + f(653)$

$(321 + 32 + 3) + (653 + 65 + 6)$

$356 + 724 = 1,080$

55

$$\frac{6x+20}{x+2} = A + \frac{B}{x+2}$$

Based on the expression above, find A+B?

A) 14

B) 20

C) 26

D) 28

$\frac{6x+20}{x+2} = \frac{A(x+2)}{(x+2)} + \frac{B}{x+2}$

$\frac{6x+20}{x+2} = \frac{A(x+2)+B}{x+2}$

$6x+20 = A(x+2) + B$

$6x+20 = Ax + 2A + B$

$A = 6$ $2A+B = 20$

$2·6+B = 20$

$12+B = 20$

$B = 8$ $A+B=14$

56

$$a+3 = b+4 = k$$

$$\frac{1}{a+3} + \frac{1}{b+4} = 1$$

Based on the equations above, what is the value of $a + b$?

A) -1

B) -2

C) -3

D) -4

$\frac{1}{a+3} + \frac{1}{b+4} = 1$ $a+3 = 2$

$\frac{1}{k} + \frac{1}{k} = 1$ $+ b+4 = 2$

                                    $a+b+7 = 4$

$\frac{2}{k} = 1$ $k = 2$ $a+b = -3$

57

$$\frac{m-1}{m-3} = \frac{m-5}{m-4}$$

According to the equation above what is the value of m?

A) $\frac{8}{5}$

B) $\frac{13}{4}$

C) $\frac{9}{4}$

D) $\frac{11}{3}$

$\frac{m-1}{m-3} = \frac{m-5}{m-4}$

$(m-1)(m-4) = (m-3)·(m-5)$

$m^2 - 4m - m + 4 = m^2 - 5m - 3m + 15$

$m^2 - 5m + 4 = m^2 - 8m + 15$

$3m = 11$

$m = \frac{11}{3}$

CONTINUE ▶

58

$$\frac{5x}{x-3}+\frac{2x}{2x-6}=\frac{54}{3x-9}$$

What value of x satisfies the equation given above?

A) 3

B) 6

C) There is no solution.

D) There are infinitely many solutions.

$$\frac{5x}{x-3}+\frac{2x}{2x-6}=\frac{54}{3x-9}$$

$$\frac{5x}{x-3}+\frac{2\cdot x}{2(x-3)}=\frac{3\cdot18}{3\cdot(x-3)}$$

$$\frac{6x}{x-3}=\frac{18}{x-3}\qquad x\neq3$$

$$\frac{6x}{6}=\frac{18}{6}\qquad x=3 \qquad \text{There is no solution}$$

59

Let $x=\dfrac{a+1}{a-3}$, what is $x-1$ in terms of a?

A) $\dfrac{2a-2}{a-3}$

B) $\dfrac{4}{a-3}$

C) $\dfrac{a}{a-3}$

D) $\dfrac{a+1}{a-4}$

$$x-1=\frac{a+1}{a-3}-1$$

$$x-1=\frac{a+1}{a-3}-\frac{a-3}{a-3}$$

$$x-1=\frac{a+1-a+3}{a-3}$$

$$x-1=\frac{4}{a-3}$$

60

$$\frac{1+\frac{1}{x}}{\frac{1}{x^2}-1}$$

What is the simplified form of the equation above?

A) $\dfrac{1}{x-1}$

B) $\dfrac{1}{1-x}$

C) $\dfrac{-x}{x-1}$

D) $\dfrac{x-1}{x}$

$$\frac{1+\frac{1}{x}}{\frac{1}{x^2}-1}=\frac{\frac{x}{x}+\frac{1}{x}}{\frac{1}{x^2}-\frac{x^2}{x^2}}$$

$$=\frac{\frac{x+1}{x}}{\frac{1-x^2}{x^2}}$$

$$=\frac{x+1}{x}\cdot\frac{x^2}{1-x^2}$$

$$=\frac{x+1}{x}\cdot\frac{x\cdot x}{(1-x)(1+x)}$$

$$=\frac{x}{1-x}=\frac{-x}{x-1}$$

61

$$\frac{5(k+2)-4}{6}=\frac{8-(3-k)}{3}$$

What is the value of k in the equation above?

A) $\dfrac{12}{21}$

B) $\dfrac{4}{3}$

C) $\dfrac{3}{2}$

D) $\dfrac{16}{3}$

$$\frac{5(k+2)-4}{6}=\frac{8-(3-k)}{3}$$

$$\frac{5k+10-4}{6}=\frac{8-3+k}{3}$$

$$\frac{5k+6}{6}=\frac{(5+k)\cdot2}{(3)\cdot2}$$

$$\frac{5k+6}{6}=\frac{10+2k}{6}$$

$$5k+6=10+2k$$

$$-2k\quad -6 \qquad -6\quad -2k$$

$$\frac{3k}{3}=\frac{4}{3}$$

$$k=\frac{4}{3}$$

62

If $3^x + 3^{x+1} + 3^{x+2} = 39$, then what is 2^x?

A) 1
B) 2
C) 4
D) 8

Handwritten work:
$3^x + 3^{x+1} + 3^{x+2} = 39$
$3^x + 3^x \cdot 3^1 + 3^x \cdot 3^2 = 39$
$3^x(1 + 3^1 + 3^2) = 39$
$3^x(13) = \dfrac{39}{13}$
$3^x = 3^1$
$x = 1$

63

$$\frac{4^x}{2^x + 2^x} = 32$$

What is the value of x which satisfies the equation given above?

A) 2
B) 4
C) 6
D) 8

Handwritten work:
$\dfrac{4^x}{2^x + 2^x} = 32 \;;\; \dfrac{2^{2x}}{2^x + 2^x} = 2^5$
$\dfrac{2^{2x}}{2^1 \cdot 2^x} = 2^5 \Rightarrow 2^{2x - x - 1} = 2^5$
$2^{x-1} = 2^5$
$x - 1 = 5$
$x = 6$

64

$$2^{20} + 16^5 + 4^{10} + 32^4 + 2^{20}$$

What is the sum of the expression above?

A) 2^{20}
B) 2^{22}
C) $5 \cdot 2^{20}$
D) $5 \cdot 2^{100}$

Handwritten work:
$2^{20} + 16^5 + 4^{10} + 32^4 + 2^{20}$
$2^{20} + (2^4)^5 + (2^2)^{10} + (2^5)^4 + 2^{20}$
$2^{20} + 2^{20} + 2^{20} + 2^{20} + 2^{20}$
$5 \cdot 2^{20}$

65

If $a^3 = b^9 c^{12}$ and a, b and c are positive numbers, then what is the value of a?

A) $\dfrac{b^9 c^{12}}{3}$
B) $b^3 c^4$
C) $b^{27} c^{36}$
D) $b^6 c^9$

Handwritten work:
$\sqrt[3]{a^3} = \sqrt[3]{b^9 c^{12}}$
$a = b^{\frac{9}{3}} \cdot c^{\frac{12}{3}}$
$a = b^3 \cdot c^4$

66

$$\sqrt[4]{4^8 + \frac{4^8 - 4^{10}}{2^4}}$$

What is the result of the operation given above?

A) 4
B) 8
C) 16
D) 32

Handwritten work:
$\sqrt[4]{4^8 + \dfrac{4^8 - 4^{10}}{2^4}} = \sqrt[4]{4^8 + \dfrac{4^8 - 4^{10}}{4^2}}$
$= \sqrt[4]{4^8 + \dfrac{4^8}{4^2} - \dfrac{4^{10}}{4^2}}$
$= \sqrt[4]{4^8 + 4^6 - 4^8}$
$= 4^{\frac{6}{4}} = (2^2)^{\frac{6}{4}} = 2^3 = 8$

67

$$\sqrt{\frac{4^7 + 4^7 + 4^7 + 4^7}{2^6 + 2^6 + 2^6 + 2^6}} = A$$

According to the equation above what is the value of A?

A) 2
B) 4
C) 16
D) 64

Handwritten work:
$\sqrt{\dfrac{4^7 + 4^7 + 4^7 + 4^7}{2^6 + 2^6 + 2^6 + 2^6}} = \sqrt{\dfrac{4 \cdot 4^7}{4 \cdot 2^6}}$
$= \sqrt{\dfrac{4^1 \cdot 4^7}{4^1 \cdot 4^3}}$
$2^6 = (2^2)^3 = 4^3$
$= \sqrt{\dfrac{4^8}{4^4}}$
$= \sqrt{4^4} = 16$

68

$$a = \sqrt{2}$$
$$b = \sqrt{7}$$
$$c = \sqrt{56}$$

What is the value of $\dfrac{c}{a^3 b}$?

A) 1

B) 2

C) 7

D) $\sqrt{2}$

[handwritten: $\dfrac{\sqrt{56}}{(\sqrt{2})^3\sqrt{7}} = \dfrac{\sqrt{56}}{\sqrt{8}\cdot\sqrt{7}} = \dfrac{\sqrt{56}}{\sqrt{56}} = 1$]

69

$$x - \sqrt{2x} = 4$$

Based on the equation above, what is the value of x?

A) 6

B) 8

C) 9

D) 12

[handwritten: $x - \sqrt{2x} = 4$; $-x \quad -x$; $(-\sqrt{2x})^2 = (4-x)^2$; $2x = 16 - 8x + x^2$; $-2x \quad -2x$; $x^2 - 10x + 16 = 0$; $(x-8)(x-2)=0$; $x=8$ or $x=2$; or; you can try the options to see which one makes $\sqrt{2x}$ an integer. $x=8$]

70

$$\sqrt[x]{a}\cdot\sqrt[y]{a}$$

What is the equivalent of the expression above?

A) $\sqrt[xy]{a}$

B) $\sqrt[xy]{a^2}$

C) $\sqrt[x+y]{a^{xy}}$

D) $\sqrt[xy]{a^{x+y}}$

[handwritten: $\sqrt[x]{a^{xy}} \cdot \sqrt[y]{a^{xy}} = \sqrt[xy]{a^y \cdot a^x} = \sqrt[xy]{a^{x+y}}$]

71

$$\frac{\sqrt{108} + \sqrt{12}}{\sqrt{48}}$$

What is the result of the operation above?

A) $\sqrt{3}$

B) $3\sqrt{3}$

C) $2\sqrt{3}$

D) 2

[handwritten: $\dfrac{\sqrt{108}+\sqrt{12}}{\sqrt{48}} = \dfrac{\sqrt{9\cdot12}+\sqrt{12}}{\sqrt{4\cdot12}} = \dfrac{3\sqrt{12}+\sqrt{12}}{2\sqrt{12}} = \dfrac{4\sqrt{12}}{2\sqrt{12}} = 2$]

72

$$a + b = 4$$
$$b - c = 3$$

What is the value of $ab - ac + b^2 - bc$?

A) 4

B) 8

C) 12

D) 16

[handwritten: $ab - ac + b^2 - bc$; $a(b-c) + b(b-c)$; $(b-c)\cdot(a+b)$; $3 \cdot 4 = 12$]

73

$$\frac{(x-2)^2(x+2)}{(x-2)}$$

Which of the following is equivalent to the expression above?

A) $-(x-2)^2$

B) $x^2 - 2x - 4$

C) $x^2 + 2x + 4$

D) $x^2 - 4$

[handwritten: $\dfrac{(x-2)^2\cdot(x+2)}{(x-2)} = \dfrac{(x-2)(x-2)(x+2)}{(x-2)} = x^2 - 4$]

CONTINUE ▶

74

$$(3a^2 - ab - 2) - (4a^2 - ab + 5)$$

Which of the following is equivalent to the expression above?

A) $-a^2 - 7$ $(3a^2-ab-2)-(4a^2-ab+5)$

B) $-a^2 + 3$ $3a^2-ab-2-4a^2+ab-5$

C) $7a^2 - 2ab + 3$ $\boxed{-a^2-7}$

D) $-a^2 - 2ab + 3$

75

If $a = 3x^2 - x + 2$, $b = x^2 + 5$, $c = 4x - 7$, then find $2a - (3b + c)$?

A) $2x^2 - 5x - 10$ $2(3x^2-x+2)-(3(x^2+5)+4x-7)$

B) $3x^2 + 2x - 18$ $6x^2-2x+4-(3x^2+15+4x-7)$

C) $3x^2 - 6x - 4$ $6x^2-2x+4-3x^2-15-4x+7$

D) $9x^2 + 2x + 12$ $\boxed{3x^2-6x-4}$

76

If $x^2 + mx + n = (x - 2)(x + 6)$, what is the value of mn?

A) -48 $x^2+mx+n = (x-2)(x+6)$

B) -12 $x^2+mx+n = x^2+6x-2x-12$

C) 4 $x^2+ mx +n = x^2 + 4x -12$

D) 24

$m=4$ $n=-12$

$m\cdot n = 4\cdot-12 = \boxed{-48}$

77

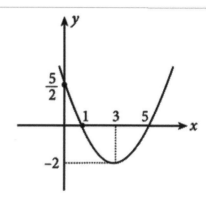

Which of the following represents the parabola shown above?

A) $f(x) = \dfrac{1}{2}(x - 3)^2 - 2$

B) $f(x) = \dfrac{1}{2}(x + 3)^2 + \dfrac{5}{2}$

C) $f(x) = (x - 3)^2 + \dfrac{5}{2}$

D) $f(x) = (x + 2)^2 + 3$

Vertex form; $f(x) = a(x-h)^2 +k$

$\boxed{f(x) = a(x-3)^2-2}$

78

$$y = -4x^2 + 16x$$

How many solutions does the quadratic equation given above have?

A) There is only one solution.
B) There are two solutions.
C) There is no solution.
D) It can not be determined.

$$-4x^2 + 16x = 0$$
$$4x(-x+4) = 0$$

x=0 $-x+4 = 0$
           $+x$ $+x$
                  $x = 4$

79

If $P(x) = ax^2 + bx + c$ and $P(1) = 8$, $P(-1) = 6$, then find the value of $a + c$.

A) 7
B) 10
C) 14
D) 48

$P(1) = a(1)^2 + b(1) + c = 8$
$a + b + c = 8$

$P(-1) = a(-1)^2 + b(-1) + c = 6$
$a - b + c = 6$

$a + b + c = 8$
$+ \quad a - b + c = 6$
_____
$\dfrac{2a + 2c}{2} = \dfrac{14}{2}$ $a + c = 7$

80

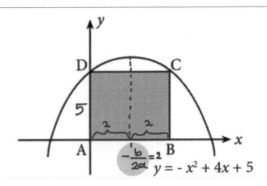

$y = -x^2 + 4x + 5$

Given the graph and formula of the parabola above, what is the area of the rectangle ABCD?

$y(0) = -0^2 + 4 \cdot 0 + 5 = 5$

A) 16
B) 20
C) 25
D) 36

$-\dfrac{b}{2a} = \dfrac{-4}{-2} = 2$

5   4   Area = 5x4 = 20

CONTINUE ▶

TEST DIRECTION

DIRECTIONS

Read the questions carefully and then choose the ONE best answer to each question.

Be sure to allocate your time carefully so you are able to complete the entire test within the testing session. You may go back and review your answers at any time.

You may use any available space in your test booklet for scratch work.

Questions in this booklet are not actual test questions but they are the samples for commonly asked questions.

This test aims to cover all topics which may appear on the actual test. However some topics may not be covered.

Studying this booklet will be preparing you for the actual test. It will not guarantee improving your test score but it will help you pass your exam on the first attempt.

Some useful tips for answering multiple choice questions;

- Start with the questions that you can easily answer.

- Underline the keywords in the question.

- Be sure to read all the choices given.

- Watch for keywords such as NOT, always, only, all, never, completely.

- Do not forget to answer every question.

CONTINUE ▶

1

Two triangles are similar. The sides of the first triangle are 5, 9, and 12. The biggest side of the second triangle is 36. Find the perimeter of the second triangle?

A) 26

B) 42

C) 64

D) 78

2

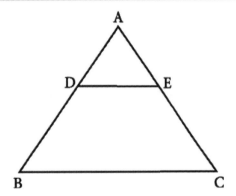

Based on the triangles above which of the following ratios is NOT true if DE is parallel to BC?

A) $\dfrac{AD}{AB} = \dfrac{AE}{AC}$

B) $\dfrac{DE}{BC} = \dfrac{AD}{AB}$

C) $\dfrac{BC}{DE} = \dfrac{AC}{AE}$

D) $\dfrac{AD}{DE} = \dfrac{AB}{AC}$

3

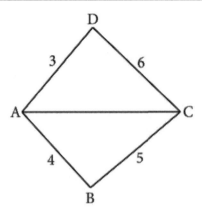

Based on the figure above, which of the following can be the length of AC?

A) 3

B) 4

C) 11

D) 12

4

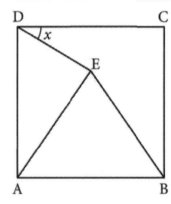

ABCD is a square and $\triangle$EAB is an equilateral triangle. What is the measure of angle x?

A) 10

B) 15

C) 20

D) 30

5

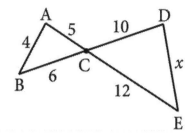

According to the figure given above what is the length of x ?

A) 2

B) 4

C) 6

D) 8

6

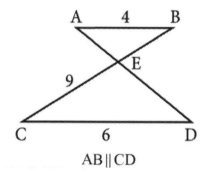

$AB \parallel CD$

Similar triangles are given above. If AB is parallel to CD, what is the length of BE?

A) 4

B) 5

C) 6

D) 10

7

An empty tank in the shape of a right circular cone has a radius of r feet and height of h feet. The tank is filled with water at a flow rate of f cubic feet per second. Which of the following expressions in terms of r, h and f gives the number of minutes to fill the tank?

A) $\dfrac{\pi r^2 h}{3f}$

B) $3\pi r^2 h$

C) $\dfrac{\pi r^2 h}{180f}$

D) $20\pi r^2 h$

8

Jashua's rectangular pencil box is 9 inches by 12 inches. What is the longest pencil that Jashua can put in his pencil box?

A) 3

B) 12

C) 15

D) 21

CONTINUE ▶

9

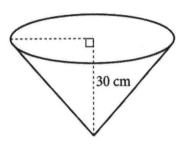

The right circular cone given above has a volume of 5,760π cubic centimeters. What is the diameter, in centimeters, of the base of the cone?

A) 12

B) 24

C) 36

D) 48

10

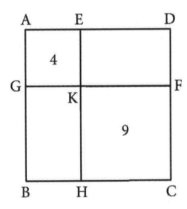

ABCD, AEKG and KFCH are squares. Area of AEKG is 4 square meters and area of KFCH is 9 square meters. What is the area of ABCD in square meters?

A) 25

B) 28

C) 32

D) 36

11

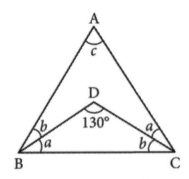

In the triangle above what is the sum of the values of the angles $a + b + c$?

A) 40

B) 50

C) 80

D) 130

12

Which of the following dimensions of a rectangular solid will have a volume closest to the right circular cylinder that has a radius of 4 and a height of 5?

A) 4,5,6

B) 4,6,7

C) 5,6,7

D) 5,6,8

13

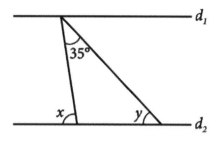

In the figure above d_1 is parallel to d_2. Which of the following expression is true?

A) $x + y = 90$

B) x is 35 degree greater then y

C) x is less then y

D) $x + y = 35$

14

A vertical flagpole casts a shadow 15 feet long at the same time that a nearby tree which is 12 feet casts a shadow 4 feet long. Find the height of the flagpole in feet?

A) 5

B) 15

C) 30

D) 45

15

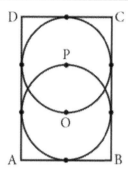

Points P and O are the centers of the circles each of which are tangent to the rectangle ABCD at three points. If the area of each circle is 64π, then what is the area of ABCD?

A) 128

B) 192

C) 384

D) 512

16

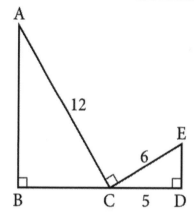

Given two similar triangles above, what is the length of AB?

A) 8

B) 9

C) 10

D) 11

17

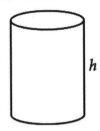

The radius of the cylinder shown above is half of its height. Which of the following is the formula of volume of this cylinder in terms of π and h?

A) $\dfrac{\pi h^3}{4}$

B) $4\pi h^3$

C) $\dfrac{\pi h^2}{2}$

D) πh^3

18

What is the volume of the cube that has a surface area of $96a^{10}$?

A) $4a^5$
B) $12a^5$
C) $16a^{10}$
D) $64a^{15}$

19

A rectangle that has longer side of 20 cm and shorter side of 5 cm is rotated around its longer side by 180 degrees and creates a semicylinder. What will be the volume of that semicylinder in cubic centimeters?

A) 250π
B) 500π
C) $1,000\pi$
D) $2,000\pi$

20

At a particular time of the day, the shadow of a 6' tree is 8' long. The shadow of a building at this same time is 48' long. How tall is the building?

A) 14
B) 24
C) 36
D) 64

21

If $\angle A$ has a measure of $\dfrac{5\pi}{4}$, what is the measure of $\angle A$, in degrees?

A) 45°

B) 90°

C) 135°

D) 225°

22

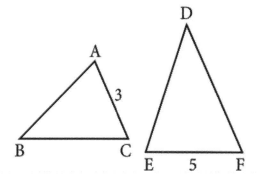

In the figure given above $\triangle ABC$ is similar to $\triangle FDE$. If circumference of $\triangle ABC$ is 36 inches, then what is the perimeter of $\triangle FDE$?

A) 12

B) 36

C) 48

D) 60

23

A farmer uses a storage silo that is in the shape of a right circular cylinder. If the volume of the silo is 144π cubic inches and the height of the silo is 9 inches, what is the radius of the base of the cylinder, in inches?

A) 2

B) 3

C) 4

D) 6

24

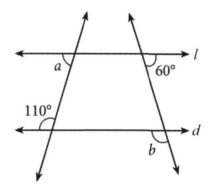

In the figure above, lines l and d are parallel. What is the value of sum of the angles $a + b$?

A) 70

B) 120

C) 170

D) 190

92

CONTINUE ▶

25

If the volume of a cube is equal to the total surface area of that cube, then what is the length of one side of the cube?

A) 6

B) 36

C) 108

D) 216

27

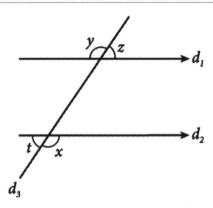

Line d_1 is parallel to d_2. If $t + z = 110$, what is $x + y$?

A) 70

B) 110

C) 200

D) 250

26

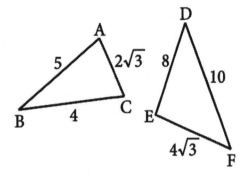

Two triangles $\triangle ABC$ and $\triangle DEF$ are shown above. If the area of $\triangle ABC = a$ cm², then what is the area of $\triangle DEF$, in terms of a?

A) a

B) $2a$

C) $3a$

D) $4a$

28

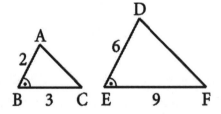

Given the triangles above $\angle ABC = \angle DEF$.

What is the value of $\dfrac{DF}{AC}$?

A) 2

B) $\dfrac{5}{2}$

C) 3

D) $\dfrac{7}{2}$

29

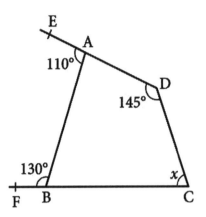

What is the measure of $\angle BCD = x$?

A) 65
B) 75
C) 85
D) 95

30

A regular rectangular prism has three different surfaces. The surface areas of different sides are 32, 40, and 80 square inches.

What is the volume of this rectangular prism in cubic inches?

A) 120
B) 240
C) 320
D) 420

31

A sphere that has a radius of r is full of water. The water is poured into a cylindirical container that has a base radius of r. What will the height of the water be in the cylindirical container in terms of r ?

A) $\dfrac{4r}{3}$

B) $\dfrac{r}{3}$

C) $2r$
D) $3r$

32

If the radius of a circle is doubled, then the area of the new circle is;

A) One-fourth of the area of the original circle.
B) One-half of the area of the original circle.
C) Two times the area of the original circle.
D) Four times the area of the original circle.

33

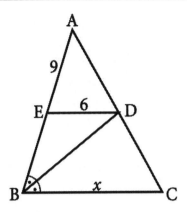

In the triangle $\triangle ABC$ given above $ED \parallel BC$.
What is the length of $BC = x$?

A) 4
B) 9
C) 10
D) 12

34

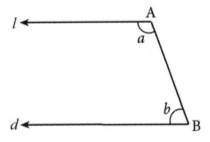

If line l is parallel to line d and, $a - b = 140$
then what is the value of b?

A) 10
B) 20
C) 30
D) 40

35

How does the volume of a cylinder change if
the radius of its base is doubled and its height
is halved?

A) The volume does not change.
B) The volume is halved.
C) The volume is doubled.
D) The volume is quadrupled.

36

A sword fish is placed in a rectangular
aquarium that has a length of 40 cm and a
width of 30 cm. If the water level rises 2 cm
when the fish is placed in the aquarium, what
is the volume of the fish in qubic centimeters?

A) 600
B) 1,200
C) 1,800
D) 2,400

37

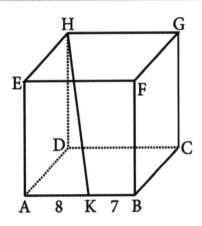

ABCDEFGH is a cube. What is the length of HK?

A) 17
B) $\sqrt{514}$
C) $5\sqrt{21}$
D) $5\sqrt{22}$

38

If a cicrle is tangent to x-axis, $y = 6$ and $x = 15$, then what is the equation of the circle?

A) $(x-15)^2 + (y-6)^2 = 9$
B) $(x-12)^2 + (y-3)^2 = 9$
C) $(x-15)^2 + (y-6)^2 = 3$
D) $(x-12)^2 + (y-6)^2 = 36$

39

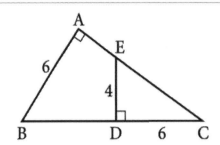

Given the triangle above, what is the length of AC?

A) 9
B) 12
C) 13
D) 15

40

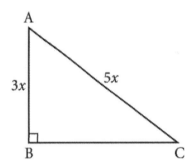

If the area of the triangle given above is 96, what is the perimeter of it?

A) 24
B) 28
C) 48
D) 96

CONTINUE ▶

41

What is the maximum number of rectangular blocks measuring 4 inches by 3 inches by 2 inches that can be packed into a cube-shaped box whose interior measures 12 inches on edge?

A) 24

B) 36

C) 72

D) 144

42

If the total surface area of a cube is 96 square feet, what is the volume of the cube in cubic feet?

A) 4

B) 16

C) 64

D) 256

43

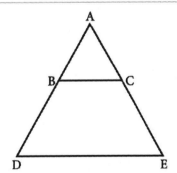

If BC is parallel to DE, $2AB = 3DB$ and $BC + DE = 40$ then what is the length of DE?

A) 15
B) 20
C) 25
D) 30

44

A circle in the xy-plane has a diameter with endpoints (-4,6) and (2,2). Which of the following is the equation of this circle?

A) $(x-1)^2 + (y+4)^2 = \sqrt{13}$

B) $(x+1)^2 + (y-4)^2 = 13$

C) $(x-4)^2 + (y-6)^2 = 13$

D) $(x-2)^2 + (y-2)^2 = 13$

45

If the diameter of a circle is $4x+2$ inches, then what is the area of the circle in square inches?

A) $(2x+1)\pi$

B) $(4x^2+1)\pi$

C) $(4x^2+4x+1)\pi$

D) $(16x^2+16x+4)\pi$

46

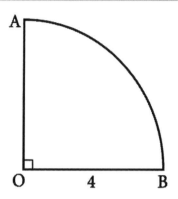

The figure above is rotated $180°$ around AO. What is the volume of the shape created by the rotation ?

A) $\dfrac{64\pi}{12}$

B) $\dfrac{64\pi}{3}$

C) $\dfrac{128\pi}{3}$

D) $\dfrac{256\pi}{3}$

47

A rectangular prism has side lengths of a, $2b$ and $3a$. In terms of a and b, what is the total surface area of the rectangular prism?

A) $16ab + 6a^2$

B) $8ab + 3a^2$

C) $14ab + 6a^2$

D) $16ab + 12a^2$

48

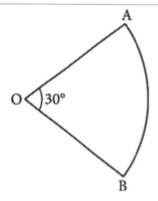

The figure above is $30°$ segment of the circle whose center is O. If the arc length of AB is 6π, then what is the radius OB of the circle?

A) 6

B) 12

C) 36

D) 72

49

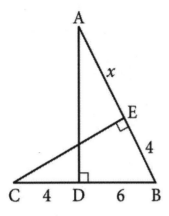

Given the triangles above, what is the length of AE = x?

A) 8

B) 9

C) 10

D) 11

50

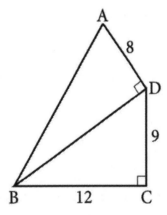

BDA and BCD are right triangles. What is the lehgth of AB?

A) 13

B) 15

C) 17

D) 23

51

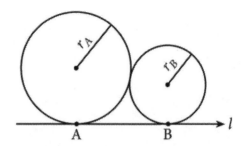

Line l is tangent to the circles at the points A and B. If AB = 12 inches, then what is the value of multiplication of the radiuses of the circles?

A) 12

B) 18

C) 36

D) 72

52

A rectangular cake has an area of 36 square unit. It has a length that is 4 unit bigger than its width. Which of the following equations can be used to find width, w, of the cake?

A) $2w + 2(w+4) = 36$

B) $4w^2 = 36$

C) $w(w-4) = 36$

D) $w(w+4) = 36$

CONTINUE ▶

53

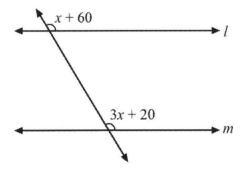

In the figure given above, a line intersects with two parallel lines of *l* and *m*. What is the value of x ?

A) 20

B) 25

C) 30

D) 40

54

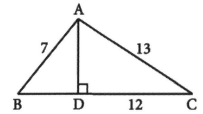

If AC=13 and DC=12, then what is the length of BD?

A) 2

B) $3\sqrt{2}$

C) $2\sqrt{6}$

D) 24

55

Which of the following can be the lengths of a right triangle?

A) $2\sqrt{2},6,2\sqrt{7}$

B) $\sqrt{2},5,\sqrt{3}$

C) 2,4,3

D) $\sqrt{5},\sqrt{41},4$

56

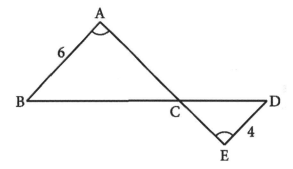

The angles ∠BAC and ∠CED are equal. If the length of BD = 20, then what is the length of CD?

A) 6

B) 8

C) 10

D) 12

100

CONTINUE ▶

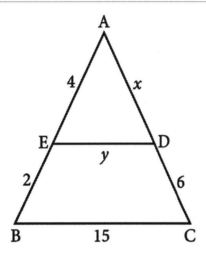

Given that $\triangle AED$ is similar with $\triangle ABC$. Find the value of $x + y$?

A) 10
B) 12
C) 15
D) 22

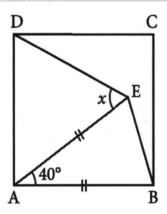

## 58

ABCD is a square and AE=AB. If $\angle EAB = 40°$ then what is the value of $\angle AED$?

A) 30
B) 50
C) 65
D) 80

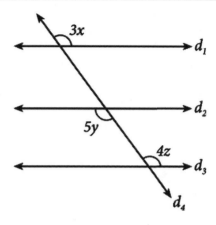

In the figure above lines d_1, d_2 and d_3 are parallel and d_4 intersects with all of the lines. Based on the angles given in the figure which of the following is true?

A) $x < z < y$
B) $z < y < x$
C) $y < z < x$
D) $y < x < z$

60

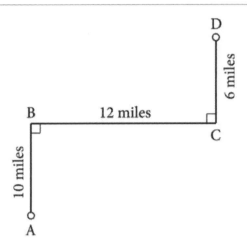

The figure above shows the route of Alfred from his house to his gym. He drives 10 miles from A to B, 12 miles from B to C and 6 miles from C to D. If he was able to drive directly from A to D, how many miles shorter would he drive?

A) 8

B) 20

C) 28

D) 48

61

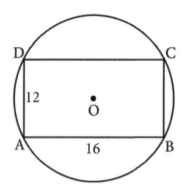

A 12 inch by 16 inch rectangle is inscribed in a circle as shown above. What is the area of the circle in square inches?

A) 100π

B) 196π

C) 256π

D) 400π

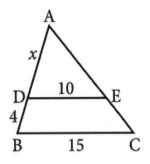

Given that DE ∥ BC, what is the value of AD= x ?

A) 6
B) 8
C) 10
D) 12

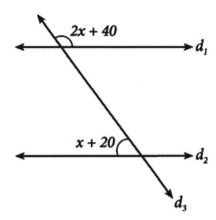

In the figure above line d_1 is parallel to the line d_2 and line d_3 intersects those lines. Based on the angles given in the figure what is the measure of x in degrees?

A) 10
B) 20
C) 30
D) 40

CONTINUE ▶

64

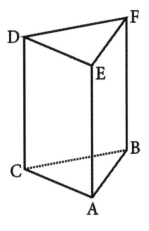

A right equilateral prism, ABCDEF is given above. If AB=6cm and BF=15cm, what is the volume of the prism, in cm³?

A) $90\sqrt{3}$

B) $135\sqrt{3}$

C) $270\sqrt{3}$

D) $540\sqrt{3}$

65

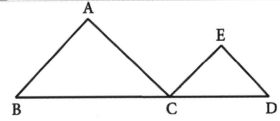

$\triangle ABC$ and $\triangle ECD$ are equilateral triangles. B, C, and D are collinear and BD = 15. What is the sum of the perimeters of the triangles?

A) 15

B) 27

C) 30

D) 45

66

	Length	Height	Width
A	4cm	8cm	3cm
B	6cm	12cm	4cm

Measures of objects A and B are given in the table above. If both objects are made of the same material what would be the weight of object B in terms of object A?

A) Two times lighter

B) The same weight

C) Three times heavier

D) Four times heavier

67

$$x^2 + y^2 + 4x + 6y = 7$$

A circle is given by the equation above. Which of the following is true about this circle?

A) The center of this circle is (2,3)

B) The radius of the circle is 7

C) The area of the circle is 20π

D) The circumference of the circle is 6π

68

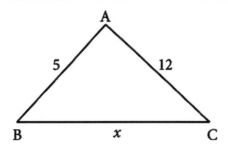

If $\angle BAC < 90°$, then which of the following can be the length of $BC = x$?

A) 7

B) 9

C) 13

D) 14

69

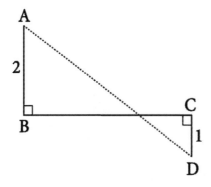

AB is perpendicular to BC and BC is perpendicular to DC. If AB=2 inch, DC=1 and BC=4 inch, what is the distance AD between the points A and D?

A) $2\sqrt{5}$

B) $2\sqrt{6}$

C) 5

D) $4\sqrt{2}$

70

How many right angles are formed by the edges of a cube?

A) 16

B) 20

C) 24

D) 30

71

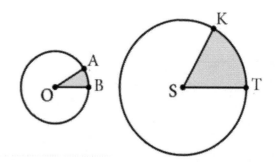

Two circles are given above. The radius of the circle with center S is three times the radius of the circle with center O, and the measure of angle KST is twice that of angle AOB. If the area of the shaded region of the circle with the center O is 10π, what is the area of the shaded region of circle with the center S?

A) 18π

B) 30π

C) 90π

D) 180π

72

ΔABC is an isoscales triangle. AB = 3x - 2 , BC = 2x + 4 , and AC = x + 5. If AB = BC, then what is the perimeter of this triangle?

A) 16

B) 25

C) 37

D) 43

73

$$K : \frac{x}{y} \qquad L : \frac{100x}{y}$$

$$M : \frac{x}{100y} \qquad N : 100xy$$

A wheel has a radius of x centimeters and a second wheel has a radius of y centimeters. The first wheel covers a distance of d centimeters in 100 revolutions. How many revolutions should the second wheel make to cover the same distance d?

A) K

B) L

C) M

D) N

74

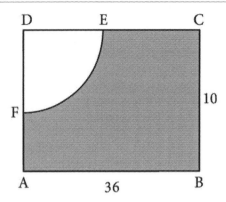

ABCD is a rectangle, DEF is a quarter circle and DE=0.5 EC. What is the area of the shaded region?

A) 360 - 144π

B) 360 - 72π

C) 360 - 36π

D) 360 - 12π

75

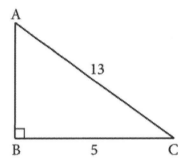

The right triangle ΔABC given above is rotated about AB and creates a cone. What is the volume of that cone?

A) 56.3π

B) 100π

C) 240π

D) 300π

76

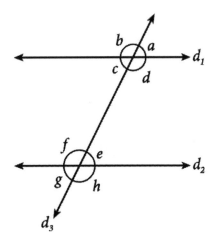

In the figure above d_1 is parallel to d_2 and d_3 intersects both lines. Which of the following can be a false statement?

A) $e = c$
B) $h = b$
C) $d = e$
D) $f = d$

77

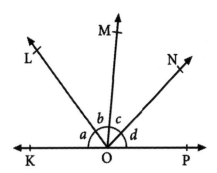

If $a + c = 80$ and $b - d = 40$, then what is the value of angle d?

A) 20
B) 30
C) 60
D) 80

78

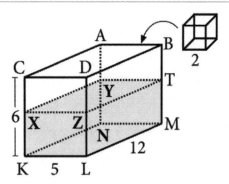

In the water tank of a rectangular prism given above, width, length, and height are 5cm, 12 cm and 6 cm. XYZT shows the water level in the tank. If MT=2BT, at most how many cubes of size 2cm can be placed into the tank such that there will be no overflow?

A) 8
B) 15
C) 30
D) 45

79

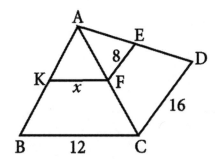

Given $\triangle ABC$ and $\triangle ACD$, $KF \parallel BC$ and $FE \parallel DC$, what is the length of $KF = x$?

A) 5
B) 6
C) 7
D) 8

80

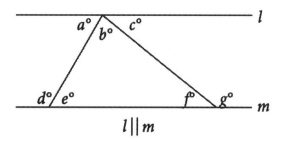

$l \parallel m$

Given the figure above, which of the following is NOT true?

A) $d = b + c$
B) $a + f = e + c$
C) $g - a = b$
D) $a + c = 540 - g - d$

81

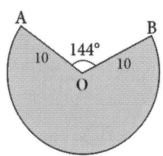

The figure above shows the surface area of a cone. What is the volume of this cone?

A) $\dfrac{32\pi\sqrt{21}}{15}$

B) $\dfrac{32\pi\sqrt{21}}{3}$

C) 96π

D) $\dfrac{160\pi}{3}$

82

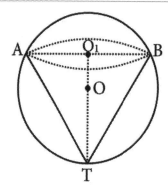

A circular cone is inscribed in a sphere with center O. If diameter of base of the cone, AB, is 24 inches, height of the cone, TO1 is 18 inches and O is also center of gravity of triangle ABT, then how many inches is the radius of the sphere?

A) 10.4

B) 13.4

C) 15.2

D) 17

CONTINUE ▶

83

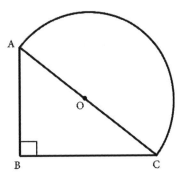

The figure above is a right triangle and a semicircle whose center is O. If AB= 6 and BC=8, what is the area of the figure?

A) $24 + 25\pi$

B) $48 + 25\pi$

C) $12 + \dfrac{25\pi}{2}$

D) $24 + \dfrac{25\pi}{2}$

84

If each side of a cube is increased by 10%, how does the volume of the cube change?

A) The volume also increases by 10%

B) The volume also increases by 21%

C) The volume also increases by 30%

D) The volume also increases by 33.1%

85

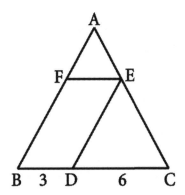

In the triangle $\triangle ABC$ given above $FE \parallel BC$ and $ED \parallel AB$. Based on the legths given on the figure what is the length of EC if $AC = 15$?

A) 6

B) 8

C) 10

D) 12

86

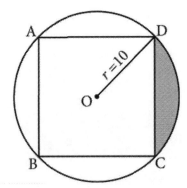

In the figure given above, the square ABCD is inscribed in a circle of r = 10. What is the area of the shaded region?

A) 25π - 50

B) 100π - 200

C) 100π

D) 200π

109

CONTINUE ▶

87

If the measure of two angles add up to 90 degrees the angles are called "**complementary angles**".

What is the measure of an angle, if five is subtracted from twice the complement and the result is 55 degrees?

A) 30

B) 55

C) 60

D) 65

88

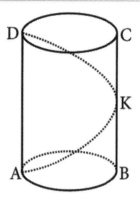

An ant starts moving from point A on the right circular cylinder, passes from point K, and reaches to the point D which is just above the point A. If the radius of the circular base of the cylinder is 4 inches, and its height is 6π, then what is the shortest distance that the ant covered?

A) 8π

B) 9π

C) 10π

D) 12π

89

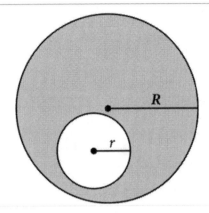

In the figure above the radius of the bigger circle is R and the radius of the smaller circle is r. If sum of the circumferences of the circles is 32π inches and the difference of the areas of the circles is 32π square inches, then what is the radius of the bigger circle, R, in inches?

A) 6

B) 7

C) 9

D) 18

90

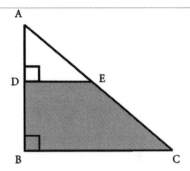

In the figure above DE is parallel to BC and $\dfrac{DE}{BC} = \dfrac{2}{3}$. If the area of $\triangle$ ADE is 84cm^2, find the area of DECB.

A) 42

B) 96

C) 105

D) 126

91

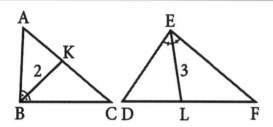

Given that $\triangle ABC \sim \triangle DEF$, BK and EL are angle bisectors. If area of $\triangle DEF = 12$ cm², what is the area of $\triangle ABC$?

A) $\dfrac{4}{3}$

B) $\dfrac{8}{3}$

C) $\dfrac{16}{3}$

D) 9

92

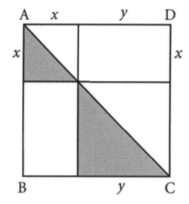

ABCD is a square. If $x + y = 7$ and $xy = 3$, then what is the shaded area?

A) 10

B) 21

C) 21.5

D) 24.5

93

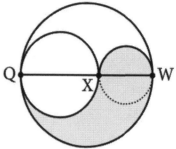

Note: Figure not drawn to scale.

QX, XW and QW are the diameters of the three circles given above. If XW = 4 inches, and QX = 2XW what is the area of the shaded region in square inches?

A) 10π

B) 12π

C) 18π

D) 24π

94

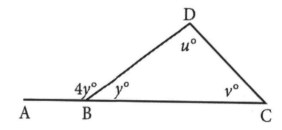

Given the figure above, if $u - v = 26$, then what is the value of v?

A) 26

B) 36

C) 59

D) 85

95

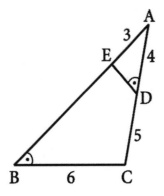

In the figure shown above $\angle ABC = \angle ADE$. Based on the given lengths, what is the length of $BE + ED$?

A) 11
B) 13
C) 15
D) 17

96

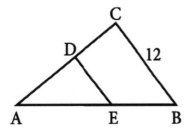

If $DE \parallel CB$ and 2EB=AE, then what is the length of DE?

A) 4
B) 5
C) 6
D) 8

97

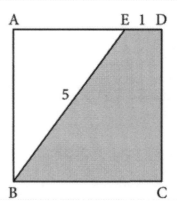

If ABCD is a square, then what is the shaded area of the square based on the given lengths of BE=5 and ED=1?

A) 6
B) 10
C) 12
D) 14

98

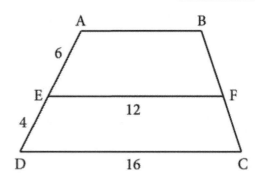

In the figure above EF is parallel to AB and DC. What is the lenght of AB?

A) 4
B) 6
C) 8
D) 10

Which of the following expresses the area A
of a circle in terms of its circumference C
and radius r ?

A) $\dfrac{C}{2}r$

B) Cr

C) $4Cr$

D) $\dfrac{C^2}{r}$

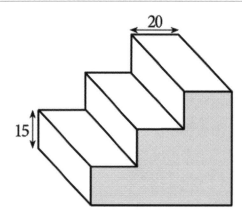

A portable ladder is shown above. Height of
each step of the ladder is 15cm, length of each
step is 20cm and width of the ladder is 60cm.
What is the volume of this portable ladder, in
cubic meter?

A) 0.054

B) 0.108

C) 0.162

D) 0.216

SECTION 3 - GEOMETRY

#	Answer	Topic	Subtopic	#	Answer	Topic	Subtopic	#	Answer	Topic	Subtopic	#	Answer	Topic	Subtopic
1	D	TD	S3	26	D	TD	S3	51	C	TD	S6	76	C	TD	S4
2	D	TD	S3	27	D	TD	S4	52	D	TD	S2	77	B	TD	S4
3	B	TD	S4	28	C	TD	S3	53	A	TD	S4	78	B	TD	S1
4	B	TD	S4	29	D	TD	S4	54	C	TD	S2	79	B	TD	S3
5	D	TD	S3	30	C	TD	S1	55	A	TD	S2	80	D	TD	S4
6	C	TD	S3	31	A	TD	S1	56	B	TD	S3	81	C	TD	S1
7	C	TD	S1	32	D	TD	S6	57	D	TD	S3	82	B	TD	S1
8	C	TD	S2	33	C	TD	S3	58	C	TD	S4	83	D	TD	S2
9	D	TD	S1	34	B	TD	S4	59	C	TD	S4	84	D	TD	S1
10	A	TD	S2	35	C	TD	S1	60	A	TD	S2	85	C	TD	S3
11	D	TD	S4	36	D	TD	S1	61	A	TD	S2	86	A	TD	S6
12	D	TD	S1	37	B	TD	S1	62	B	TD	S3	87	C	TD	S4
13	B	TD	S4	38	B	TD	S6	63	D	TD	S4	88	C	TD	S1
14	D	TD	S3	39	A	TD	S3	64	B	TD	S1	89	C	TD	S6
15	C	TD	S6	40	C	TD	S2	65	D	TD	S3	90	C	TD	S3
16	C	TD	S3	41	C	TD	S1	66	C	TD	S1	91	C	TD	S3
17	A	TD	S1	42	C	TD	S4	67	C	TD	S6	92	C	TD	S2
18	D	TD	S1	43	C	TD	S3	68	B	TD	S4	93	B	TD	S6
19	A	TD	S1	44	B	TD	S6	69	C	TD	S2	94	C	TD	S4
20	C	TD	S3	45	C	TD	S6	70	C	TD	S1	95	A	TD	S3
21	D	TD	S4	46	B	TD	S1	71	D	TD	S6	96	D	TD	S3
22	D	TD	S3	47	A	TD	S1	72	D	TD	S4	97	B	TD	S2
23	C	TD	S1	48	C	TD	S6	73	B	TD	S6	98	B	TD	S3
24	D	TD	S4	49	D	TD	S3	74	C	TD	S6	99	A	TD	S6
25	A	TD	S1	50	C	TD	S2	75	B	TD	S1	100	B	TD	S1

Topics & Subtopics

Code	Description	Code	Description
SD1	Volume & Surface Area	SD4	Angles & Triangles
SD2	Right Triangles	SD6	Circles & Arc Length
SD3	Congruence & Similarity	TD	Additional Topics in Math

CONTINUE ▶

1

Two triangles are similar. The sides of the first triangle are 5, 9, and 12. The biggest side of the second triangle is 36. Find the perimeter of the second triangle?

A) 26

B) 42

C) 64

D) 78

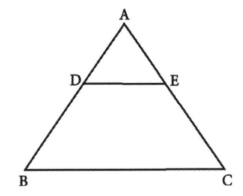

2

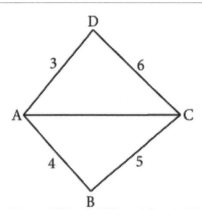

Based on the triangles above which of the following ratios is NOT true if DE is parallel to BC?

A) $\dfrac{AD}{AB} = \dfrac{AE}{AC}$

B) $\dfrac{DE}{BC} = \dfrac{AD}{AB}$

C) $\dfrac{BC}{DE} = \dfrac{AC}{AE}$

D) $\dfrac{AD}{DE} = \dfrac{AB}{AC}$

3

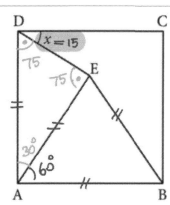

Based on the figure above, which of the following can be the length of AC?

A) 3

B) 4

C) 11

D) 12

4

ABCD is a square and ΔEAB is an equilateral triangle. What is the measure of angle x?

A) 10

B) 15

C) 20

D) 30

116

CONTINUE ▶

5

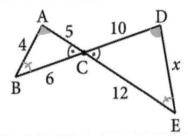

According to the figure given above what is the length of *x* ?

$\triangle ABC \sim \triangle DEC$

A) 2

B) 4

C) 6

D) 8

$\frac{4}{x} = \frac{5}{10}$ $\frac{5x}{5} = \frac{4 \cdot 10}{5}$

$x = 8$

6

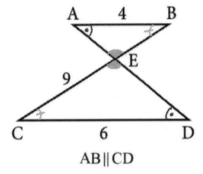

AB∥CD

Similar triangles are given above. If AB is parallel to CD, what is the length of BE?

A) 4 $\triangle AEB \sim \triangle DEC$

B) 5

C) 6 $\frac{4}{6} = \frac{BE}{9}$ $\frac{6 \times BE}{6} = \frac{4 \times 9}{6}$

D) 10

$BE = 6$

7

An empty tank in the shape of a right circular cone has a radius of *r* feet and height of *h* feet. The tank is filled with water at a flow rate of *f* cubic feet per second. Which of the following expressions in terms of *r*, *h* and *f* gives the number of minutes to fill the tank?

rate = 60f cubic feet per minute

A) $\dfrac{\pi r^2 h}{3f}$

B) $3\pi r^2 h$

C) $\dfrac{\pi r^2 h}{180f}$

D) $20\pi r^2 h$

$60f \cdot \frac{t}{60f} = \frac{1}{3} \frac{\pi r^2 h}{60f}$

$t = \frac{\pi r^2 h}{180f}$

8

Jashua's rectangular pencil box is 9 inches by 12 inches. What is the longest pencil that Jashua can put in his pencil box?

A) 3 $\ell^2 = 9^2 + 12^2$

B) 12 $\ell^2 = 81 + 144$

C) 15 $\sqrt{\ell^2} = \sqrt{225}$ $\ell = 15$

D) 21

9

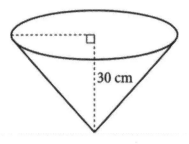

The right circular cone given above has a volume of 5,760π cubic centimeters. What is the diameter, in centimeters, of the base of the cone?

$5,760\pi = \frac{1}{3} \cdot \pi \cdot r^2 \cdot 30$

A) 12

B) 24

C) 36

D) 48

$\sqrt{r^2} = \sqrt{576}$

$r = 24$

diameter $= 2 \cdot r = 2 \cdot 24 = 48$

10

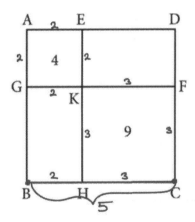

ABCD, AEKG and KFCH are squares. Area of AEKG is 4 square meters and area of KFCH is 9 square meters. What is the area of ABCD in square meters?

A) 25 $\sqrt{4} = 2$ side of AEKG

B) 28 $\sqrt{9} = 3$ "

C) 32 $5^2 = 25$ is the area of ABCD

D) 36

11

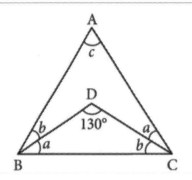

In the triangle above what is the sum of the values of the angles $a + b + c$?

$130 + a + b = 180$ $a + b = 50$
$\qquad -130 \qquad\qquad -130$

A) 40

B) 50 $c + 2a + 2b = 180$
$\qquad\quad c + 2 \cdot 50 = 180 \quad c + 100 = 180$

C) 80 $\qquad\qquad\qquad\qquad -100 \quad -100$

D) 130 $\qquad\qquad\qquad\qquad\quad c = 80$

$a + b + c = 50 + 80 = 130$

12

Which of the following dimensions of a rectangular solid will have a volume closest to the right circular cylinder that has a radius of 4 and a height of 5?

$\pi r^2 h = \pi \cdot 4^2 \cdot 5 = 80\pi \approx 240$

A) 4,5,6 → 120

B) 4,6,7 → 168

C) 5,6,7 → 210

D) 5,6,8 → 240

13

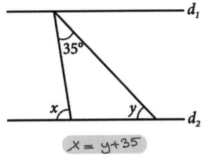

$$x = y + 35$$

In the figure above d_1 is parallel to d_2. Which of the following expression is true?

A) $x + y = 90$

B) x is 35 degree greater then y

C) x is less then y

D) $x + y = 35$

14

A vertical flagpole casts a shadow 15 feet long at the same time that a nearby tree which is 12 feet casts a shadow 4 feet long. Find the height of the flagpole in feet?

A) 5

B) 15

C) 30

D) 45

$$\frac{12}{4} = \frac{h}{15}$$

$$\frac{4 \times h}{4} = \frac{12 \times 15}{4}$$

$$h = 45$$

15

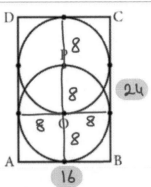

Points P and O are the centers of the circles each of which are tangent to the rectangle ABCD at three points. If the area of each circle is 64π, then what is the area of ABCD?

A) 128

B) 192

C) 384

D) 512

$$64\pi = \pi r^2 \qquad r = 8$$

$$16 \times 24 = 384$$

16

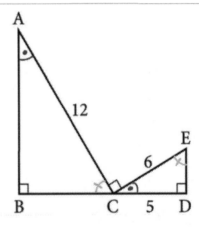

Given two similar triangles above, what is the length of AB?

$$\triangle BAC \sim \triangle DCE$$

A) 8

B) 9

C) 10

D) 11

$$\frac{5}{AB} = \frac{6}{12} \qquad \frac{6 AB}{6} = \frac{5 \times 12}{6}$$

$$AB = 10$$

17

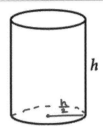

The radius of the cylinder shown above is half of its height. Which of the following is the formula of volume of this cylinder in terms of π and h?

A) $\dfrac{\pi h^3}{4}$ $\pi r^2 h = \pi\left(\dfrac{h}{2}\right)^2 \cdot h = \boxed{\dfrac{\pi h^3}{4}}$

B) $4\pi h^3$

C) $\dfrac{\pi h^2}{2}$

D) πh^3

18

What is the volume of the cube that has a surface area of $96a^{10}$?

A) $4a^5$ $\dfrac{6x^2}{6} = \dfrac{96a^{10}}{6}$ $V = x^3$

B) $12a^5$

C) $16a^{10}$ $\sqrt{x^2} = \sqrt{16a^{10}}$ $V = (4a^5)^3$

D) $64a^{15}$ $x = 4a^5$ $V = \boxed{64a^{15}}$

19

A rectangle that has longer side of 20 cm and shorter side of 5 cm is rotated around its longer side by 180 degrees and creates a semicylinder. What will be the volume of that semicylinder in cubic centimeters?

A) 250π $V = \dfrac{\pi r^2 h}{2} = \dfrac{\pi \cdot 5^2 \cdot 20}{2}$

B) 500π

C) $1,000\pi$ $V = \boxed{250\pi}$

D) $2,000\pi$

20

At a particular time of the day, the shadow of a 6' tree is 8' long. The shadow of a building at this same time is 48' long. How tall is the building?

A) 14 $\dfrac{6}{8} = \dfrac{x}{48}$ $\dfrac{8 \cdot x}{8} = \dfrac{6 \cdot 48}{8}$

B) 24

C) 36 $x = \boxed{36}$

D) 64

CONTINUE ▶

21

If $\angle A$ has a measure of $\dfrac{5\pi}{4}$, what is the measure of $\angle A$, in degrees?

A) 45°
B) 90°
C) 135°
D) 225°

$5 \cdot \dfrac{\pi}{4} = 5 \cdot \dfrac{180}{4} = \boxed{225}$

22

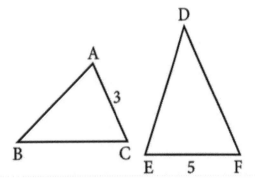

In the figure given above $\triangle ABC$ is similar to $\triangle FDE$. If circumference of $\triangle ABC$ is 36 inches, then what is the perimeter of $\triangle FDE$?

A) 12   Ratio of similarity = Ratio of perimeter
B) 36 $\dfrac{3}{5} = \dfrac{36}{x}$ $\dfrac{3 \cdot x}{3} = \dfrac{5 \cdot 36}{3}$
C) 48
D) 60 $x = 60$

23

A farmer uses a storage silo that is in the shape of a right circular cylinder. If the volume of the silo is 144π cubic inches and the height of the silo is 9 inches, what is the radius of the base of the cylinder, in inches?

$V = \pi r^2 h$

A) 2
B) 3 $\dfrac{144\pi}{9} = \dfrac{\pi r^2 \cdot 9}{9}$ $\sqrt{r^2} = \sqrt{16}$
C) 4 $r = 4$
D) 6

24

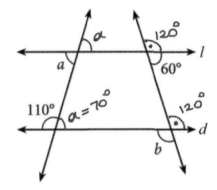

In the figure above, lines l and d are parallel. What is the value of sum of the angles $a + b$?

A) 70 $a + b = 70 + 120 = \boxed{190}$
B) 120
C) 170
D) 190

25

If the volume of a cube is equal to the total surface area of that cube, then what is the length of one side of the cube?

A) 6 $\dfrac{a^3}{a^2} = \dfrac{6a^2}{a^2}$ $a = 6$

B) 36

C) 108

D) 216

26

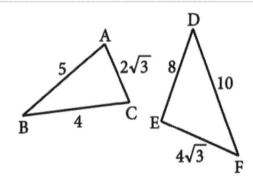

Two triangles $\triangle ABC$ and $\triangle DEF$ are shown above. If the area of $\triangle ABC = a$ cm², then what is the area of $\triangle DEF$, in terms of a?

A) a similarity ratio $= \dfrac{4}{8} = \dfrac{5}{10} = \dfrac{2\sqrt{3}}{4\sqrt{3}} = \dfrac{1}{2}$

B) $2a$

C) $3a$ (similarity ratio)² = Ratio of areas

D) $4a$

$\left(\dfrac{1}{2}\right)^2 = \dfrac{a}{x}$ $\dfrac{1}{4} = \dfrac{a}{x}$

$x = 4a$

27

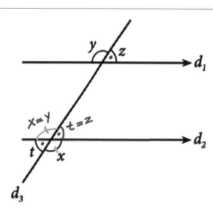

Line d_1 is parallel to d_2. If $t + z = 110$, what is $x + y$?

$t + z = t + t = \dfrac{2t}{2} = \dfrac{110}{2}$

$t = 55$

A) 70

B) 110 $x + t = 180$ $x + 55 = 180$

C) 200 $-55 \quad -55$

D) 250 $x + y = x + x = 2x = 2 \times 125 = 250$ $x = 125$

28

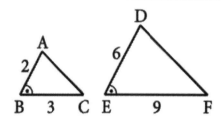

Given the triangles above $\angle ABC = \angle DEF$.

What is the value of $\dfrac{DF}{AC}$?

A) 2

B) $\dfrac{5}{2}$ $\triangle ABC \sim \triangle DEF$

C) 3 $\dfrac{DF}{AC} = \dfrac{9}{3} = 3$

D) $\dfrac{7}{2}$

122   **CONTINUE ▶**

29

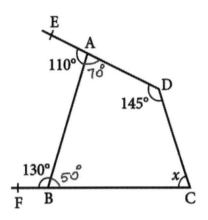

What is the measure of $\angle BCD = x$?

A) 65 $50+70+145+x = 360$

B) 75 $\quad\quad 265 +x = 360$

C) 85 $\quad\quad -265 \quad\quad -265$

D) 95 $\boxed{x = 95}$

30

A regular rectangular prism has three different surfaces. The surface areas of different sides are 32, 40, and 80 square inches.

What is the volume of this rectangular prism in cubic inches?

$a \times b = 32$

$a \times c = 40$

A) 120 $x \quad b \times c = 80$

B) 240 $\overline{(a \times b \times c)^2 = 32 \times 40 \times 80}$

C) 320 $a \times b \times c = \sqrt{32 \times 32 \times 100}$

D) 420 $\boxed{a \times b \times c = 320}$

31

A sphere that has a radius of r is full of water. The water is poured into a cylindirical container that has a base radius of r. What will the height of the water be in the cylindirical container in terms of r ?

A) $\dfrac{4r}{3}$ $\dfrac{4}{3}\pi r^3 \dfrac{}{\pi r^2} = \dfrac{\pi r^2 h}{\pi r^2}$

B) $\dfrac{r}{3}$ $\boxed{h = \dfrac{4r}{3}}$

C) $2r$

D) $3r$

32

If the radius of a circle is doubled, then the area of the new circle is;

A) One-fourth of the area of the original circle.

B) One-half of the area of the original circle.

C) Two times the area of the original circle.

D) Four times the area of the original circle.

$A = \pi r^2 \quad A = \pi (2r)^2 = 4\pi r^2$

33

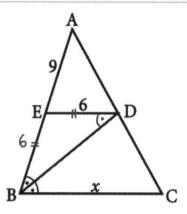

In the triangle $\triangle ABC$ given above $ED \parallel BC$.
What is the length of $BC = x$?

A) 4
B) 9
C) 10
D) 12

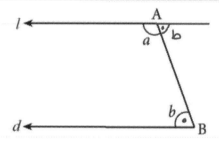

$\triangle AED \sim \triangle ABC$

$\dfrac{9}{9+6} = \dfrac{6}{x}$ $\dfrac{9}{15} = \dfrac{6}{x}$

$\dfrac{9x}{9} = \dfrac{6 \cdot 15}{9}$ $x = 10$

34

If line *l* is parallel to line *d* and, $a - b = 140$
then what is the value of *b*?

A) 10
B) 20
C) 30
D) 40

$a + b = 180$
$+ \ \ -a + b = -140$
$\dfrac{2b}{2} = \dfrac{40}{2}$
$b = 20$

35

How does the volume of a cylinder change if
the radius of its base is doubled and its height
is halved?

A) The volume does not change.
B) The volume is halved.
C) The volume is doubled.
D) The volume is quadrupled.

$V = \pi r^2 h$ $V = \pi (2r)^2 \cdot \dfrac{h}{2}$

$V = 2\,\pi r^2 h$

36

A sword fish is placed in a rectangular
aquarium that has a length of 40 cm and a
width of 30 cm. If the water level rises 2 cm
when the fish is placed in the aquarium, what
is the volume of the fish in qubic centimeters?

A) 600 $V = 40 \times 30 \times 2 = 2,400 \, cm^3$
B) 1,200
C) 1,800
D) 2,400

37

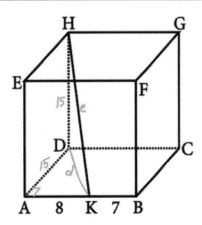

ABCDEFGH is a cube. What is the length of HK?

$d^2 = 8^2 + 15^2 = 64 + 225 = 289$

$e^2 = d^2 + 15^2 = 289 + 225 = 514$

A) 17

B) $\sqrt{514}$

C) $5\sqrt{21}$

D) $5\sqrt{22}$

$\sqrt{e^2} = \sqrt{514}$

$e = \sqrt{514}$

38

If a cicrle is tangent to x-axis, $y = 6$ and $x = 15$, then what is the equation of the circle?

A) $(x-15)^2 + (y-6)^2 = 9$

B) $(x-12)^2 + (y-3)^2 = 9$

C) $(x-15)^2 + (y-6)^2 = 3$

D) $(x-12)^2 + (y-6)^2 = 36$

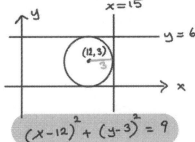

$(x-12)^2 + (y-3)^2 = 9$

39

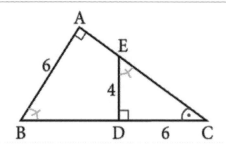

Given the triangle above, what is the length of AC?

$\triangle ABC \sim DEC$

A) 9

B) 12

C) 13

D) 15

$\dfrac{6}{4} = \dfrac{AC}{6}$

$\dfrac{4AC}{4} = \dfrac{6 \cdot 6}{4}$

$AC = 9$

40

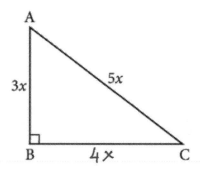

If the area of the triangle given above is 96, what is the perimeter of it?

A) 24

B) 28

C) 48

D) 96

is a special triangle

$\frac{1}{2} \cdot 3x \cdot 4x = 96$

$\dfrac{6x^2}{6} = \dfrac{96}{6}$

$\sqrt{x^2} = \sqrt{16}$

$x = 4$

$3x + 4x + 5x = 12x$

Perimeter $= 12 \cdot 4 = 48$

CONTINUE ▶

41

What is the maximum number of rectangular blocks measuring 4 inches by 3 inches by 2 inches that can be packed into a cube-shaped box whose interior measures 12 inches on edge?

A) 24

B) 36

C) 72

D) 144

$$\frac{12 \times 12 \times 12}{4 \times 3 \times 2} = 72$$

42

If the total surface area of a cube is 96 square feet, what is the volume of the cube in cubic feet?

A) 4

B) 16

C) 64

D) 256

$$\frac{6a^2}{6} = \frac{96}{6}$$
$$\sqrt{a^2} = \sqrt{16}$$
$$a = 4 \qquad V = a^3$$
$$V = 4^3 = 64$$

43

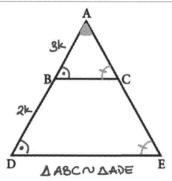

$$\triangle ABC \sim \triangle ADE$$

If BC is parallel to DE, $2AB = 3DB$ and $BC + DE = 40$ then what is the length of DE ?

A) 15

B) 20

C) 25

D) 30

$$\frac{BC}{DE} = \frac{3k}{5k} \qquad BC + DE = 40$$
$$3k + 5k = 40$$
$$\frac{8k}{8} = \frac{40}{8}$$
$$k = 5$$
$$DE = 5k = 5 \cdot 5 = 25$$

44

A circle in the xy-plane has a diameter with endpoints $(-4,6)$ and $(2,2)$. Which of the following is the equation of this circle ?

A) $(x-1)^2 + (y+4)^2 = \sqrt{13}$

B) $(x+1)^2 + (y-4)^2 = 13$

C) $(x-4)^2 + (y-6)^2 = 13$

D) $(x-2)^2 + (y-2)^2 = 13$

$$C = \left(\frac{-4+2}{2}, \frac{6+2}{2}\right)$$
$$C = (-1, 4)$$
$$r^2 = (2-(-1))^2 + (2-4)^2$$
$$r^2 = 3^2 + (-2)^2 = 13$$
$$(x-(-1))^2 + (y-4)^2 = 13$$

45

If the diameter of a circle is $4x+2$ inches, then what is the area of the circle in square inches?

A) $(2x+1)\pi$

B) $(4x^2+1)\pi$

C) $(4x^2+4x+1)\pi$

D) $(16x^2+16x+4)\pi$

$r = \frac{4x+2}{2} = 2x+1$

$A = \pi r^2 = \pi (2x+1)^2$

$A = \pi(4x^2+4x+1)$

46

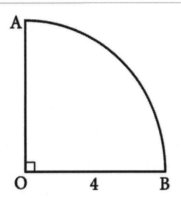

The figure above is rotated $180°$ around AO. What is the volume of the shape created by the rotation ?

A) $\dfrac{64\pi}{12}$

B) $\dfrac{64\pi}{3}$

C) $\dfrac{128\pi}{3}$

D) $\dfrac{256\pi}{3}$

$\frac{1}{4}$ of a sphere will be created.

$\frac{1}{4} \cdot \frac{4}{3}\pi \cdot 4^3 = \frac{64\pi}{3}$

47

A rectangular prism has side lengths of a, $2b$ and $3a$. In terms of a and b, what is the total surface area of the rectangular prism?

A) $16ab+6a^2$

B) $8ab+3a^2$

C) $14ab+6a^2$

D) $16ab+12a^2$

$2\left[(a \cdot 2b)+(a \cdot 3a)+(2b \cdot 3a)\right]$

$2\left[2ab+3a^2+6ab\right]$

$2\left[8ab+3a^2\right]$

$16ab+6a^2$

48

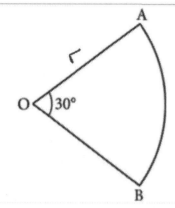

The figure above is $30°$ segment of the circle whose center is O. If the arc length of AB is 6π, then what is the radius OB of the circle?

A) 6

B) 12

C) 36

D) 72

$2\pi r \cdot \frac{30°}{360°} = 6\pi$

$\frac{2\pi r}{12} = 6\pi \cdot 6$

$r = 36$

CONTINUE ▶

49

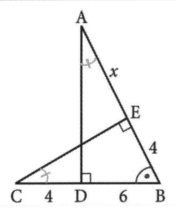

Given the triangles above, what is the length of AE = x?

$\triangle DAB \sim \triangle ECB$

$\frac{6}{4} = \frac{x+4}{10}$

$60 = 4x+16$
$-16 \qquad -16$

$\frac{44}{4} = \frac{4x}{4}$

$x = 11$

A) 8

B) 9

C) 10

D) 11

50

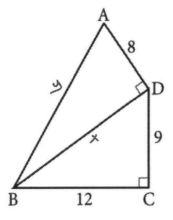

BDA and BCD are right triangles. What is the lehgth of AB?

A) 13

B) 15

C) 17

D) 23

$x^2 = 9^2 + 12^2$
$x^2 = 81+144$
$x^2 = 225$

$x^2 + 8^2 = y^2$
$225+64 = y^2$
$\sqrt{289} = \sqrt{y^2}$

$y = 17$

51

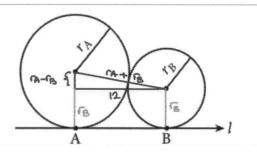

Line l is tangent to the circles at the points A and B. If AB = 12 inches, then what is the value of multiplication of the radiuses of the circles?

A) 12

B) 18

C) 36

D) 72

$(\sqrt{r_A} + \sqrt{r_B})^2 = (\sqrt{r_A} - \sqrt{r_B})^2 + 12^2$

$r_A^2 + r_B^2 + 2\sqrt{r_A}\sqrt{r_B} = r_A^2 + r_B^2 - 2\sqrt{r_A}\sqrt{r_B} + 144$

$+2\sqrt{r_A}\sqrt{r_B} \qquad\qquad +2\sqrt{r_A}\sqrt{r_B}$

$\frac{4\sqrt{r_A}\sqrt{r_B}}{4} = \frac{288}{4}$

$\sqrt{r_A}\cdot\sqrt{r_B} = 72$

52

A rectangular cake has an area of 36 square unit. It has a length that is 4 unit bigger than its width. Which of the following equations can be used to find width, w, of the cake?

A) $2w+2(w+4)=36$

B) $4w^2=36$

C) $w(w-4)=36$

D) $w(w+4)=36$

$l = w+4$

$l \cdot w = 36$

$(w+4) \cdot w = 36$

128

CONTINUE ▶

53

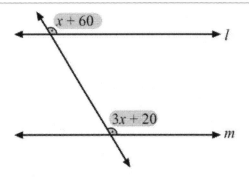

In the figure given above, a line intersects with two parallel lines of *l* and *m*. What is the value of *x* ?

A) 20

$x+60 = 3x+20$
$-x \quad -20 \quad -x \quad -20$

B) 25

$\dfrac{40}{2} = \dfrac{2x}{2}$

C) 30

$x = 20$

D) 40

54

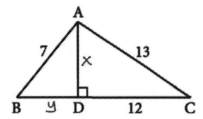

If AC=13 and DC=12, then what is the length of BD?

A) 2

$x^2+y^2=7^2 \qquad x^2+12^2=13^2$
$5^2+y^2=49 \qquad x^2+144=169$

B) 3√2

$25+y^2=49 \qquad -144 \quad -144$

C) 2√6

$\sqrt{y^2}=\sqrt{24} \qquad \sqrt{x^2}=\sqrt{25}$
$-25 \qquad -25 \qquad x=5$

D) 24

$y=\sqrt{4\cdot6}=2\sqrt{6}$

55

Which of the following can be the lengths of a right triangle? Biggest side will be the hypotenuse;

A) $2\sqrt{2},6,2\sqrt{7}$

$6^2=(2\sqrt{2})^2+(2\sqrt{7})^2 \qquad 5^2=(\sqrt{2})^2+(\sqrt{3})^2$
$36=4\cdot2+4\cdot7 \qquad 25\neq5$
$36=36$ ✓

B) $\sqrt{2},5,\sqrt{3}$

$4^2=3^2+2^2 \qquad (\sqrt{41})^2=(\sqrt{5})^2+4^2$

C) 2,4,3

$16\neq13 \qquad 41\neq21$

D) $\sqrt{5},\sqrt{41},4$

56

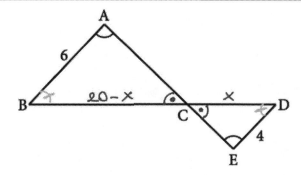

The angles ∠BAC and ∠CED are equal. If the length of BD = 20, then what is the length of CD?

$\triangle ABC \sim \triangle EDC$

A) 6

$\dfrac{4}{6}=\dfrac{x}{20-x} \qquad 80-4x=6x$

B) 8

$+4x \qquad +4x$

C) 10

$\dfrac{10x}{10}=\dfrac{80}{10}$

D) 12

$x=8$

57

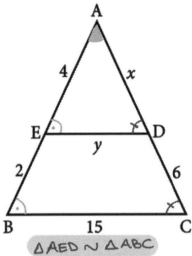

$\triangle AED \sim \triangle ABC$

Given that $\triangle AED$ is similar with $\triangle ABC$. Find the value of $x + y$?

$\frac{y}{15} = \frac{x}{x+6} = \frac{4}{4+2}$

A) 10
B) 12
C) 15
D) 22

$\frac{4}{6} = \frac{y}{15}$ and $\frac{4}{6} = \frac{x}{x+6}$

$\frac{6y}{6} = \frac{4 \cdot 15}{6}$

$y = 10$

$4x + 24 = 6x$

$-4x \qquad -4x$

$\frac{2x}{2} = \frac{24}{2}$

$x = 12$

$x + y = 22$

58

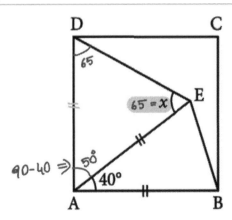

ABCD is a square and AE = AB. If $\angle EAB = 40°$ then what is the value of $\angle AED$?

A) 30
B) 50
C) 65
D) 80

AD is equal to AE, then

$\angle ADE = \angle AED$

$\frac{180 - 50}{2} = 65°$

59

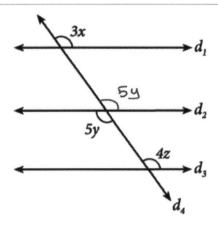

In the figure above lines d_1, d_2 and d_3 are parallel and d_4 intersects with all of the lines. Based on the angles given in the figure which of the following is true?

A) $x < z < y$
B) $z < y < x$
C) $y < z < x$
D) $y < x < z$

$3x = 4z = 5y$

$x > z > y$

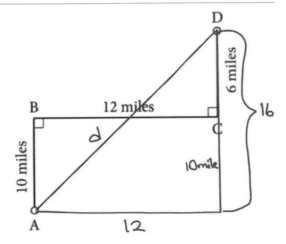

The figure above shows the route of Alfred from his house to his gym. He drives 10 miles from A to B, 12 miles from B to C and 6 miles from C to D. If he was able to drive directly from A to D, how many miles shorter would he drive?

A) 8

$d^2 = 12^2 + 16^2$ or   use special

B) 20

$d^2 = 144 + 256$ triangle

C) 28

$\sqrt{d^2} = \sqrt{400}$

D) 48

$d = 20$mile

$(10 + 12 + 6) - 20 = $ 8 miles

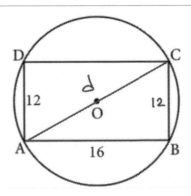

A 12 inch by 16 inch rectangle is inscribed in a circle as shown above. What is the area of the circle in square inches?

A) 100π

$d^2 = 12^2 + 16^2$ or   use special

B) 196π

$d^2 = 144 + 256$ triangle

C) 256π

$\sqrt{d^2} = \sqrt{400}$

D) 400π

$d = 20$

$r = 10$

$\pi r^2 = \pi \cdot 10^2 = $ 100π

131

CONTINUE ▶

62

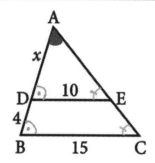

Given that DE ∥ BC, what is the value of AD=x?

A) 6
B) 8
C) 10
D) 12

$\triangle ADE \sim \triangle ABC$

$\dfrac{10}{15} = \dfrac{x}{x+4}$

$10x+40 = 15x$
$-10x \qquad -10x$

$\dfrac{40}{5} = \dfrac{5x}{5}$

$x = 5$

63

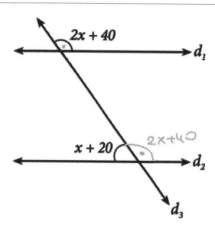

In the figure above line d_1 is parallel to the line d_2 and line d_3 intersects those lines. Based on the angles given in the figure what is the measure of x in degrees?

A) 10
B) 20
C) 30
D) 40

$x+20 + 2x+40 = 180$

$3x + 60 = 180$
$-60 \qquad -60$

$\dfrac{3x}{3} = \dfrac{120}{3}$

$x = 40$

CONTINUE ▶

64

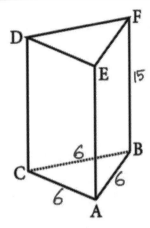

A right equilateral prism, ABCDEF is given above. If AB=6cm and BF=15cm, what is the volume of the prism, in cm³?

A) $90\sqrt{3}$ Volume = Base area × height

B) $135\sqrt{3}$ $= \frac{6^2\sqrt{3}}{4} \times 15$

C) $270\sqrt{3}$ $= \boxed{135\sqrt{3}}$

D) $540\sqrt{3}$

65

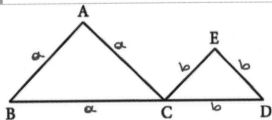

ΔABC and ΔECD are equilateral triangles. B, C, and D are collinear and BD = 15. What is the sum of the perimeters of the triangles?

$$a+b=15$$

A) 15   Sum of the perimeters $= 3a+3b$

B) 27 $= 3(a+b)$

C) 30 $= 3(15)$

D) 45 $= \boxed{45}$

66

	Length	Height	Width	Volume
A	4cm	8cm	3cm	96
B	6cm	12cm	4cm	288

Measures of objects A and B are given in the table above. If both objects are made of the same material what would be the weight of object B in terms of object A?

A) Two times lighter

B) The same weight

C) Three times heavier

D) Four times heavier

Because they are made of the same material we can compare their volumes.

$\frac{288}{96} = 3$ B is 3 times A.

67

$$x^2 + y^2 + 4x + 6y = 7$$

A circle is given by the equation above. Which of the following is true about this circle?

A) The center of this circle is (2,3)

B) The radius of the circle is 7

C) The area of the circle is 20π

D) The circumference of the circle is 6π

$(x^2+4x+4) + (y^2+6y+9) = 7+4+9$

$(x+2)^2 + (y+3)^2 = 20$

$C(-2,-3)$ $r=\sqrt{20}$

$Area = \pi r^2 = \pi(\sqrt{20})^2 = 20\pi$

68

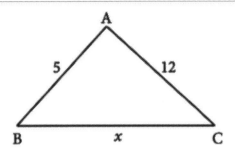

If $\angle BAC < 90°$, then which of the following can be the length of $BC = x$?

$12-5 < x < 12+5$

A) 7 $7 < x < 17$

B) 9   If $\angle BAC$ was $90°$ then;

C) 13 $x^2 = 5^2 + 12^2$ $x^2 = 169$ $x = 13$

            Because $\angle BAC < 90°$, then $x < 13$

D) 14

$7 < x < 13$

69

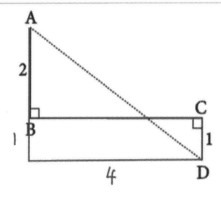

AB is perpendicular to BC and BC is perpendicular to DC. If AB=2 inch, DC=1 and BC=4 inch, what is the distance AD between the points A and D?

A) $2\sqrt{5}$ $AD^2 = 3^2 + 4^2$

B) $2\sqrt{6}$ $AD^2 = 9 + 16$

C) 5 $\sqrt{AD^2} = \sqrt{25}$

D) $4\sqrt{2}$ $AD = 5$

70

How many right angles are formed by the edges of a cube?

A) 16

B) 20   Each face of the cube

C) 24 has 4 right angles. 6 face

D) 30 has $6 \times 4 = 24$

71

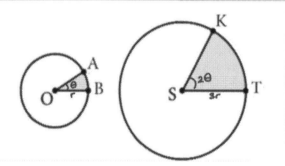

Two circles are given above. The radius of the circle with center S is three times the radius of the circle with center O, and the measure of angle KST is twice that of angle AOB. If the area of the shaded region of the circle with the center O is 10π, what is the area of the shaded region of circle with the center S?

A) 18π $\pi r^2 \cdot \dfrac{\theta}{360} = 10\pi$

B) 30π $\pi (3r)^2 \cdot \dfrac{2\theta}{360} = 18 \cdot \pi r^2 \dfrac{\theta}{360}$

C) 90π

D) 180π $= 18 \cdot 10\pi$

                         $= 180\pi$

134

CONTINUE ▶

72

$\triangle ABC$ is an isoscales triangle. $AB = 3x - 2$, $BC = 2x + 4$, and $AC = x + 5$. If $AB = BC$, then what is the perimeter of this triangle?

A) 16

B) 25

C) 37

D) 43

$3x - 2 = 2x + 4$
$-2x + 2 \quad -2x + 2$
$x = 6$
$(3 \cdot 6 - 2) + (2 \cdot 6 + 4) + (6 + 5)$
$18 - 2 + 12 + 4 + 11 = \boxed{43}$

73

$$K : \frac{x}{y} \qquad L : \frac{100x}{y}$$

$$M : \frac{x}{100y} \qquad N : 100xy$$

A wheel has a radius of x centimeters and a second wheel has a radius of y centimeters. The first wheel covers a distance of d centimeters in 100 revolutions. How many revolutions should the second wheel make to cover the same distance d?

A) K $100 \cdot 2\pi x = d = n \cdot 2\pi y$

B) L

C) M $\dfrac{100 \cdot 2\pi x}{y} = \dfrac{n \cdot 2\pi y}{y}$

D) N

$n = \dfrac{100x}{y}$

74

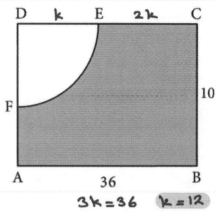

$3k = 36 \quad k = 12$

ABCD is a rectangle, DEF is a quarter circle and DE=0.5 EC. What is the area of the shaded region?

A) $360 - 144\pi$

B) $360 - 72\pi$ $36 \cdot 10 - \frac{1}{4}\pi \cdot 12^2$

C) $360 - 36\pi$ $360 - 36\pi$

D) $360 - 12\pi$

75

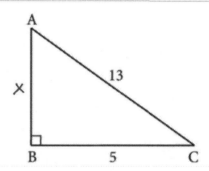

The right triangle $\triangle ABC$ given above is rotated about AB and creates a cone. What is the volume of that cone?

A) 56.3π $x^2 + 5^2 = 13^2$ $V = \frac{1}{3}\pi r^2 h$

B) 100π $x^2 + 25 = 169$
                $-25 \quad -25$ $V = \frac{1}{3}\pi \cdot 5^2 \cdot 12$

C) 240π $\sqrt{x^2} = \sqrt{144}$

D) 300π $x = 12$ $V = 100\pi$

76

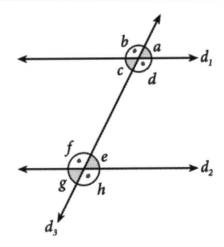

In the figure above d_1 is parallel to d_2 and d_3 intersects both lines. Which of the following can be a false statement?

A) $e = c$
B) $h = b$
C) $d = e$ 　　$d = f = 180 - e$
D) $f = d$

77

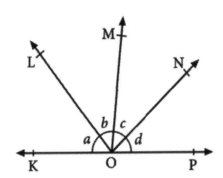

If $a + c = 80$ and $b - d = 40$, then what is the value of angle d?

$a + c = 80$
$+　b - d = 40$
$a + b + c - d = 120$

A) 20
B) 30
C) 60
D) 80

$a + b + c + d = 180$
$+　-a + b + c + d = -120$
$\frac{2d}{2} = \frac{60}{2}$

$d = 30$

78

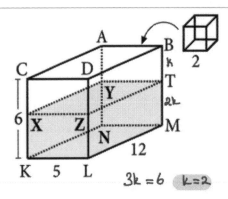

$3k = 6$　$k = 2$

In the water tank of a rectangular prism given above, width, length, and height are 5cm, 12 cm and 6 cm. XYZT shows the water level in the tank. If MT=2BT, at most how many cubes of size 2cm can be placed into the tank such that there will be no overflow?

A) 8　$\dfrac{\text{Volume of empty space}}{\text{Volume of one cube}} = \dfrac{2 \times 5 \times 12}{2 \times 2 \times 2} = 15$
B) 15
C) 30
D) 45

79

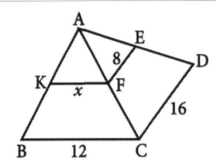

Given $\triangle ABC$ and $\triangle ACD$, $KF \parallel BC$ and $FE \parallel DC$, what is the length of $KF = x$?

A) 5　　$\dfrac{x}{12} = \dfrac{8}{16}$　　$\dfrac{12 \cdot 8}{16} = \dfrac{16 \cdot x}{16}$
B) 6
C) 7　　　　　　　　　　$x = 6$
D) 8

CONTINUE ▶

80

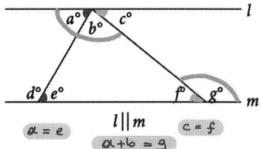

$l \parallel m$

$\alpha = e$

$a + b = g$

$c = f$

Given the figure above, which of the following is NOT true?

A) $d = b + c$ $d = b+f \; ; \; f=c \; ; \; d = b+c$

B) $a + f = e + c$ $e+f = e+f$

C) $g - a = b$ $g = a+b$

D) $a + c = 540 - g - d$

81

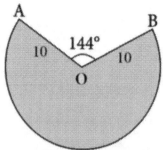

The figure above shows the surface area of a cone. What is the volume of this cone?

$2\pi r_{cone} = 2\pi \cdot 10 \cdot \dfrac{216}{360}$

A) $\dfrac{32\pi\sqrt{21}}{15}$ $r_{cone} = 6$

B) $\dfrac{32\pi\sqrt{21}}{3}$ $V_{cone} = \dfrac{1}{3}\pi r^2 h$

C) 96π $V_{cone} = \dfrac{1}{3}\pi \cdot 6^2 \cdot 8$ $10^2 = 6^2 + h^2$

$\sqrt{h^2} = \sqrt{64}$

D) $\dfrac{160\pi}{3}$ $V_{cone} = 96\pi$ $h = 8$

82

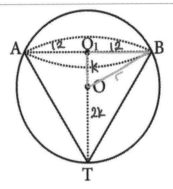

A circular cone is inscribed in a sphere with center O. If diameter of base of the cone, AB, is 24 inches, height of the cone, TO1 is 18 inches and O is also center of gravity of triangle ABT, then how many inches is the radius of the sphere?

$TO_1 = 3k$

$18 = 3k$

$k = 6$

A) 10.4

B) 13.4

C) 15.2

D) 17

$r^2 = 12^2 + 6^2$

$r^2 = 144 + 36$

$\sqrt{r^2} = \sqrt{180}$

$r = 13.4$

83

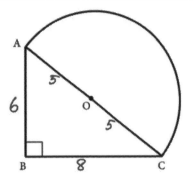

The figure above is a right triangle and a semicircle whose center is O. If AB= 6 and BC=8, what is the area of the figure?

A) $24 + 25\pi$

B) $48 + 25\pi$

C) $12 + \dfrac{25\pi}{2}$

D) $24 + \dfrac{25\pi}{2}$

Right triangle + Semicircle

$\dfrac{1}{2} \cdot 6 \cdot 8 + \dfrac{\pi \cdot 5^2}{2}$

$24 + \dfrac{25}{2}\pi$

84

If each side of a cube is increased by 10%, how does the volume of the cube change?

A) The volume also increases by 10%

B) The volume also increases by 21%

C) The volume also increases by 30%

D) The volume also increases by 33.1%

Let one side of the cube be 10, then after 10% increase it will be 11.

$V = 10 \cdot 10 \cdot 10$
$V = 1,000$

$V = 11 \cdot 11 \cdot 11$
$V = 1,331$

$\dfrac{1,331-1,000}{1,000} = 33.1\%$

85

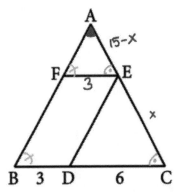

In the triangle $\triangle ABC$ given above $FE \parallel BC$ and $ED \parallel AB$. Based on the legths given on the figure what is the length of EC if $AC = 15$?

A) 6
B) 8
C) 10
D) 12

$\triangle AFE \sim \triangle ABC$

$\dfrac{3}{9} = \dfrac{15-x}{15} \Rightarrow 15 = 45 - 3x$

$\dfrac{3x}{3} = \dfrac{30}{3}$

$x = 10$

86

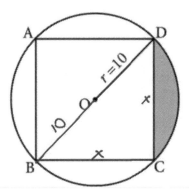

In the figure given above, the square ABCD is inscribed in a circle of r = 10. What is the area of the shaded region?

A) $25\pi - 50$

B) $100\pi - 200$

C) 100π

D) 200π

$x^2 + x^2 = 20^2 \qquad 2x^2 = 400$
$\qquad\qquad\qquad\qquad x^2 = 200$

Area of circle - Area of square

$\dfrac{\pi \cdot 10^2 - x^2}{4} = \dfrac{100\pi - 200}{4}$

$= 25\pi - 50$

87

If the measure of two angles add up to 90 degrees the angles are called "**complementary angles**".

What is the measure of an angle, if five is subtracted from twice the complement and the result is 55 degrees?

A) 30
B) 55
C) 60
D) 65

Let the angle be x, then complement will be $(90-x)$

$2 \cdot (90-x) - 5 = 55$
$\qquad\qquad\quad +5 \quad +5$

$\dfrac{2 \cdot (90-x)}{2} = \dfrac{60}{2}$

$90 - x = 30$

$x = 60$

88

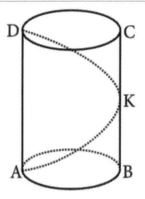

An ant starts moving from point A on the right circular cylinder, passes from point K, and reaches to the point D which is just above the point A. If the radius of the circular base of the cylinder is 4 inches, and its height is 6π, then what is the shortest distance that the ant covered?

A) 8π

B) 9π

C) 10π

D) 12π

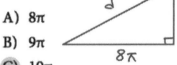

special triangle

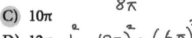

$d^2 = (8\pi)^2 + (6\pi)^2$ or;

$d^2 = 64\pi^2 + 36\pi^2$

$\sqrt{d^2} = \sqrt{100\pi^2}$

$d = 10\pi$

89

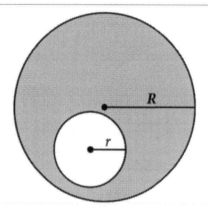

In the figure above the radius of the bigger circle is R and the radius of the smaller circle is r. If sum of the circumferences of the circles is 32π inches and the difference of the areas of the circles is 32π square inches, then what is the radius of the bigger circle, R, in inches?

A) 6 $2\pi R + 2\pi r = 32\pi \Rightarrow R + r = 16$

B) 7 $\pi R^2 - \pi r^2 = 32\pi \Rightarrow R^2 - r^2 = 32$

C) 9 $(R+r)(R-r) = 32$

D) 18 $\dfrac{16}{16} \cdot (R-r) = \dfrac{32}{16}$

$R - r = 2$

$R + r = 16$
$+ R - r = 2$
_____
$\dfrac{2R}{2} = \dfrac{18}{2}$

$R = 9$

140

CONTINUE ▶

90

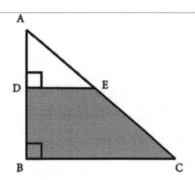

In the figure above DE is parallel to BC and
$\dfrac{DE}{BC} = \dfrac{2}{3}$. If the area of $\triangle ADE$ is 84cm², find
the area of DECB.

A) 42
B) 96
C) 105
D) 126

$\dfrac{\text{Area of } \triangle ADE}{\text{Area of } \triangle ABC} = (\text{Ratio of similarity})^2$

$\dfrac{84}{\text{Area of } \triangle ABC} = \left(\dfrac{2}{3}\right)^2 = \dfrac{4}{9}$

$\dfrac{\cancel{4} \cdot \text{Area of } \triangle ABC}{\cancel{4}} = \dfrac{9 \cdot 84}{4}$

$\text{Area of } \triangle ABC = 188$
$\text{Area of DECB} = 188 - 84 = \boxed{105}$

91

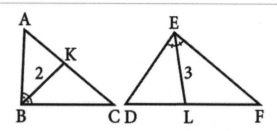

Given that $\triangle ABC \sim \triangle DEF$, BK and EL are
angle bisectors. If area of $\triangle DEF = 12$ cm², what
is the area of $\triangle ABC$?

A) $\dfrac{4}{3}$ Ratio of areas $= (\text{Ratio of similarity})^2$

B) $\dfrac{8}{3}$ $\dfrac{\text{Area of } \triangle ABC}{\text{Area of } \triangle DEF} = \left(\dfrac{2}{3}\right)^2$

C) $\dfrac{16}{3}$ $\cancel{\text{X}} \cdot \dfrac{\text{Area of } \triangle ABC}{\cancel{12}} = \dfrac{4}{9} \cdot 12$

D) 9 $\text{Area of } \triangle ABC = \dfrac{48}{9} = \boxed{\dfrac{16}{3}}$

92

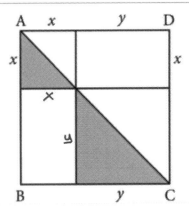

ABCD is a square. If $x + y = 7$ and $xy = 3$, then what is the shaded area?

Shaded area $= \frac{1}{2} \cdot x \cdot x + \frac{1}{2} \cdot y \cdot y$

$= \frac{x^2 + y^2}{2}$

A) 10

B) 21

C) 21.5

D) 24.5

$(x+y)^2 = (7)^2 \Rightarrow x^2 + y^2 + 2xy = 49$
$x^2 + y^2 + 2 \cdot 3 = 49$
$x^2 + y^2 = 43$

Shaded area $= \frac{43}{2} = 21.5$

94

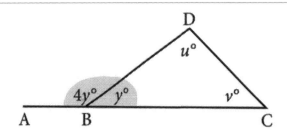

Given the figure above, if $u - v = 26$, then what is the value of v?

A) 26 $\frac{5y}{5} = \frac{180}{5}$ $\begin{aligned} u+v &= 144 \\ -u+v &= -26 \end{aligned}$

B) 36 $y = 36$

C) 59 $180 - y = u+v$ $\frac{2v}{2} = \frac{118}{2}$

D) 85 $180 - 36 = u+v$ $v = 59$

$u + v = 144$

93

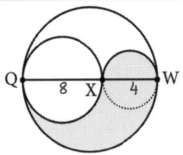

Note: Figure not drawn to scale.

QX, XW and QW are the diameters of the three circles given above. If XW = 4 inches, and QX = 2XW what is the area of the shaded region in square inches?

Shaded area $= \frac{\pi \cdot 6^2}{2} - \frac{\pi \cdot 4^2}{2} + \frac{\pi 2^2}{2}$

A) 10π

B) 12π

$= \frac{36\pi}{2} - \frac{16\pi}{2} + \frac{4\pi}{2}$

C) 18π

$= \frac{24\pi}{2} = 12\pi$

D) 24π

95

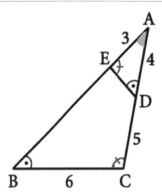

In the figure shown above $\angle ABC = \angle ADE$. Based on the given lengths, what is the length of $BE + ED$? $\triangle AED \sim \triangle ACB$

A) 11 $\frac{4}{3+BE} = \frac{3}{4+5} = \frac{DE}{6}$

B) 13 $\frac{4}{3+BE} = \frac{1}{3}$ $\frac{1}{3} = \frac{DE}{6}$

C) 15

D) 17 $12 = 3 + BE$ $\frac{6}{3} = \frac{3DE}{3}$

$BE = 9$ $DE = 2$

$BE + DE = 11$

142   **CONTINUE ▶**

96

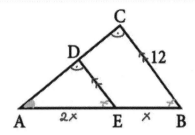

If DE ∥ CB and 2EB=AE, then what is the length of DE?

A) 4
B) 5
C) 6
D) 8

Handwritten work:
C, D, 12, A, 2x, E, x, B
x $2x$

$\triangle ADE \sim \triangle ACB$

$\dfrac{2x}{3x} = \dfrac{DE}{12}$ $\dfrac{2 \cdot 12}{3} = \dfrac{3 \cdot DE}{3}$

$DE = 8$

97

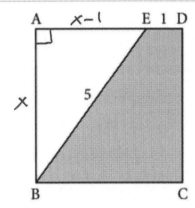

If ABCD is a square, then what is the shaded area of the square based on the given lengths of BE=5 and ED=1?

A) 6
B) 10
C) 12
D) 14

Handwritten work:
$x^2 + (x-1)^2 = 5^2$

$x^2 + x^2 - 2x + 1 = 25$

$2x^2 - 2x - 24 = 0$

$x^2 - x - 12 = 0$

$(x-4)(x+3) = 0$

$x=4$ $x=-3$

Shaded Area
$4^2 - \frac{1}{2} 4 \cdot 3$

$16 - 6 = 10$

98

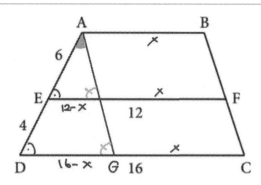

In the figure above EF is parallel to AB and DC. What is the lenght of AB?

A) 4
B) 6
C) 8
D) 10

Handwritten work:
Drawing a line from A to a point, G, on DC will create two similar triangles.

$\dfrac{6}{10} = \dfrac{12-x}{16-x}$

$96 - 6x = 120 - 10x$

$-96 + 10x \quad -96 + 10x$

$4x = 24$

$x = 6$

99

Which of the following expresses the area A of a circle in terms of its circumference C and radius r?

A) $\dfrac{C}{2}r$
B) Cr
C) $4Cr$
D) $\dfrac{C^2}{r}$

Handwritten work:
$A = \pi r^2$ $C = 2\pi r$

$\dfrac{2\pi r \cdot r}{2} = \dfrac{C}{2} \cdot r$

$\pi r^2 = \dfrac{Cr}{2}$

CONTINUE ▶

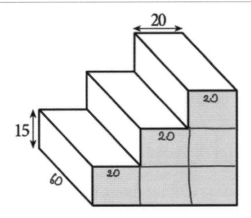

A portable ladder is shown above. Height of each step of the ladder is 15cm, length of each step is 20cm and width of the ladder is 60cm. What is the volume of this portable ladder, in cubic meter?

There are 6 rectangular prisms in the ladder.

A) 0.054

B) 0.108 $6 \times (15 \times 20 \times 60) = 108,000 \ cm^3$

C) 0.162 $(1 cm)^3 = (10^{-2} m)^3 \quad 1 cm^3 = 10^{-6} m^3$

D) 0.216 $108,000 \cdot 10^{-6} m^3 = 0.108 \ m^3$

TEST DIRECTION

DIRECTIONS

Read the questions carefully and then choose the ONE best answer to each question.

Be sure to allocate your time carefully so you are able to complete the entire test within the testing session. You may go back and review your answers at any time.

You may use any available space in your test booklet for scratch work.

Questions in this booklet are not actual test questions but they are the samples for commonly asked questions.

This test aims to cover all topics which may appear on the actual test. However some topics may not be covered.

Studying this booklet will be preparing you for the actual test. It will not guarantee improving your test score but it will help you pass your exam on the first attempt.

Some useful tips for answering multiple choice questions;

- Start with the questions that you can easily answer.

- Underline the keywords in the question.

- Be sure to read all the choices given.

- Watch for keywords such as NOT, always, only, all, never, completely.

- Do not forget to answer every question.

CONTINUE ▶

1

Employees at a Bank				
Years Worked	Teller	Manager	Supervisor	Total
Less than 5	26	12	23	61
5 to 10	19	17	12	48
10 to 15	18	15	20	53
More than 15	17	11	10	38
Total	80	55	65	200

The table above shows the years worked by employees at a bank. What is the probability that a teller has worked for 5 or more years?

A) 27%

B) 32.5%

C) 67.5%

D) 80%

2

KLMNOPRKLMNOPRKLM...

In the sequence of letters shown above, the first letter K is, followed by L, M, N, O, P and R.

Which of the following is the 41st letter in this sequence?

A) K

B) L

C) P

D) R

3

Sam has got the following grades on his tests; 78, 85, 98, and 82. He wants an 85 or better overall. What is the minimum grade Sam must get on the last test in order to achieve that average?

A) 72

B) 82

C) 85

D) 90

4

A coin with two sides, heads, and tails, is flipped 4 times and the results are recorded. What is the probability that the 3rd flip results in tails?

A) 0.063

B) 0.125

C) 0.250

D) 0.500

5

Mr. Avadis rasied all of his students' scores on a recent exam by 12 points. What effect did this increase have on the mean and median of the scores?

A) The mean and the median did not change.

B) The mean and the median increased by 12 points.

C) The mean increased by 12 points, but the median remained the same.

D) The median increased by 12 points, but the mean remained the same.

6

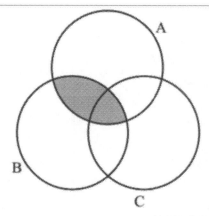

In the figure above, three circles represent single family houses on the Miami Beach. Circle A represents a house with an ocean view, Circle B represents a house with 5 bedrooms, and Circle C represents a house with a swimming pool.

What does the shaded region represent?

A) House with an ocean view, 5 bedrooms, and swimming pool

B) House with an ocean view and 5 bedrooms, but without swimming pool

C) House with an ocean view and 5 bedrooms (some possibly with swimming pool)

D) House with an ocean view and swimming pool (some possibly with 5 bedrooms)

7

$$m, 2m, n$$

If the artithemetic mean(average) of the 3 numbers given above is $2m$, then what is the value of n in terms of m?

A) $\dfrac{1}{2}m$

B) m

C) $\dfrac{3}{2}m$

D) $3m$

8

Sarah collected data on the weights of five newborn kittens. The weights of the kittens, in ounces, are; 12, 7, 6, 8, 12

Which statement regarding the mean, median, and range of the weights of the kittens is true?

A) The mean is greater than the median, and the range is 12.

B) The median is greater than the mean, and the range is 12.

C) The median is greater than the mean, and the range is 7.

D) The mean is greater than the median, and the range is 6.

9

Lengths of Fish (in inches)						
9	7	10	11	8	10	11
11	12	12	12	12	13	13
14	14	15	15	15	16	25

The lengths of a random sample of 21 fish are listed in the table given above, but the measurement of 25 inches is an error.

Which of the following would not be true when the 25-inch measurement is removed from the data?

A) Median does not change.

B) Mode does not change.

C) Mean does not change.

D) Range decreases.

10

LINCOLN HIGH SCHOOL		
	Girls	Boys
Freshman	140	120
Sophomores	110	115
Juniors	112	124
Seniors	118	111

The chart above shows the grade level of girls and boys in Lincoln High School. If a boy is chosen at random, what is the probability that he is a junior?

A) 0.233

B) 0.264

C) 0.275

D) 0.310

CONTINUE ▶

11

How many different five-member teams can be made from a group of nine players, if each player has an equal chance of being selected?

A) 36

B) 45

C) 126

D) 3,024

12

2, 4, 6, 8, 10, 12, 14, 16

If a number is chosen at random from the list given above, what is the probability that the number is divisible by 3?

A) 0.25

B) 0.33

C) 0.50

D) 0.75

13

Sales representatives realize that in Universal Studios for 100 tickets sold, toy shops sell 8 Transformer Robots at $35.00 each, 7 t-shirts of Shrek at $20.00 each, and 4 Harry Potter Illuminating Wand at $12.00 each. What is the arithmetic mean of these toy sales per ticket sold?

A) $4.28

B) $4.68

C) $5.48

D) $24.63

14

Given that there are 4 aces and 4 queens in a deck of 52 cards total, what is the probability of drawing neither an ace nor a queen from a deck of cards?

A) $\frac{2}{13}$

B) $\frac{4}{13}$

C) $\frac{8}{13}$

D) $\frac{11}{13}$

15

In the figure above, 5 parking lots are to be assigned to 5 employees; Ryan, Isabella, Mia, Giancarlo, and Cathrine. Ryan and Giancarlo are men and Isabella, Mia and Catherine are women.

The following conditions must be met:

• Parking lot 1 is assigned to a man.
• Catherine is assigned to Parking lot 5.
• Parking lot 4 is assigned to a woman.
• To each parking lot, a different employee must be assigned
• Mia is assigned to an odd-numbered parking lot and Ryan is assigned to an even-numbered Parking lot.

Which of the following employee is assigned to Parking lot 4?

A) Giancarlo
B) Ryan
C) Mia
D) Isabella

16

If m is chosen at random from the set $\{4,5,7\}$ and n is chosen at random from the set $\{9,10,11\}$, what is the probability that the product of m and n is divisible by 5?

A) $\dfrac{1}{3}$

B) $\dfrac{4}{9}$

C) $\dfrac{5}{9}$

D) $\dfrac{2}{3}$

17

Number of Students	Scores
3	90
9	80
7	70
4	65
6	55

Emily's score was accidentally omitted from the list given above. When her score is added, the arithmetic mean(average) of the class does not change. What is Emily's score?

A) 67.9

B) 69

C) 71.4

D) 72

18

In Montclair High School Mr. Alferi raised all of his students' mathematics scores on a recent exam by 12 points.

How does this increase in the scores affect the mean and the median of the scores?

A) The mean increased by 12 points, but the median remained the same.

B) The median increased by 12 points, but the mean remained the same.

C) The mean increased by 12 points, and the median increased by 12 points.

D) The mean and the median remained the same.

19

Amelia has 5 different skirts, 4 different pairs of pants, 6 different t-shirts, and 3 different jackets from which to choose when dressing for a party.

What is the total number of different combinations of 1 skirt, 1 t-shirt, 1 pair of pants, and 1 jacket?

A) 18

B) 30

C) 120

D) 360

20

If the average measure of two angles in a triangle is A, then what is the other angle of this triangle?

A) 180 - A

B) 180 - 0.5A

C) 180 - 2A

D) 360 - 2A

21

NUMBER OF EMPLOYEES		
Salary($)	Teacher	Manager
90,000 or more	30	10
Less than 90,000	90	40

The table above shows the number of employees in a school district which is classified according to personnel type and salary. If a teacher will be selected at random, what is the probability that the teacher's salary is over $90,000?

A) 0.25

B) 0.33

C) 0.50

D) 0.66

22

Employees at a School				
Years worked	Nurse	Custodian	Teacher	Total
Less than 3	8	12	120	140
3 to 5	11	10	110	131
6 to 9	10	16	180	206
More than 9	12	14	120	146
Total	41	52	530	623

The table given above shows the years worked by employees at a school district. What is the probability of selecting a custodian who has worked for 6 or more years in the district?

A) 4.8%

B) 8.3%

C) 27%

D) 57.7%

23

A bag contains 7 red, 5 yellow, and 8 orange marbles. How many red marbles must be added into the bag so that the probability of randomly drawing a red marble is 0.48?

A) 3

B) 5

C) 12

D) 33

24

The results of the survey conducted at Montville High School indicates that the median of the heights of all of the male students was 164 centimeters and the mode was 160 centimeters.

According to this information which of the following statements must be true?

A) There are no male students taller than 164 centimeters.

B) The most frequently occurring height of the male students is 160 centimeters.

C) The average (arithmetic mean) of the heights of the male students is 162 centimeters.

D) There are more male students who are 164 centimeters tall than those who are 160 centimeters tall.

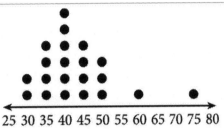

25 30 35 40 45 50 55 60 65 70 75 80

Average Flight delay (in minutes)

Length of Cables
8 feet
10 feet
x feet
9 feet
7 feet
11 feet

The average delay of flights for each of the largest 21 airline companies in Asia, was calculated and shown in the dot plot above.

If the highest flight delay is removed from the dot plot, which of the following changes occur?

A) The average will decrease only.

B) The average and median will decrease only.

C) The range and average will decrease only.

D) The median, range, and average will decrease.

A store has six different lengths of extension cables for sale. The length of the cables are shown in the table above. If the range of lengths of the six cables is 6 feet, what is the least possible value of x?

A) 5

B) 6

C) 16

D) 17

27

	Age		
Gender	Under 35	35 or older	Total
Male	14	2	16
Female	5	4	9
Total	19	6	25

The table above shows the distribution of gender and age for 25 people who have taken a medical treatment in Saint Joseph medical center in Passaic County. If one person out of these 25 people will be selected at random, what is the probability that the selected will be either a female over age 35 or a male under age 35?

A) 0.28

B) 0.56

C) 0.72

D) 0.76

28

If a fair dice is rolled twice, what is the probability that the first roll produces 3 and the second roll does NOT produce a 5?

A) 0.280

B) 0.139

C) 0.166

D) 0.333

29

The candidates for a college are ranked by their high school GPA (Grade Point Average). There is an equal number of girls and boys in the application list, but more boys than girls are in the top 50% of the list.

Based on the information given above, which of the following statement must be true?

A) The highest ranked candidate is a boy.

B) The lowest ranked candidate is a girl.

C) There are at least 20 boys in the top 50% of the class.

D) There are more girls than boys in the bottom 50% of the class.

30

College Students' Sleep Habits		
Hours of Sleep	Uphill College	Frontier College
Average	5	7
Median	3	6
Mode	4	7
Standard Deviation	4	3

A random sample of students in two different colleges were surveyed for their sleep habits. The results are shown in the table below.

Which of the following statements is supported by the data given in this table?

A) More students attend Frontier College than Uphill College.

B) Variation of the hours of sleep per night among students at Uphill College is more than that of students' at Frontier College.

C) Less than half of the students at Uphill College get 6 hours of sleep per night.

D) More than half of the students at Uphill College get 5 hours of sleep per night.

31

SCHOOL FURNITURE SETS			
Set	K	L	M
Desk	1	2	4
Chairs	6	5	2

PRICES			
Year	2002	2007	2012
Desk	$70	$80	$100
Chairs	$20	$40	$60

A school furniture company sells three sets of furnitures; set K, set L and set M. Each collection consists of a different number of tables and chairs as shown in the first table above. The second table given below the first one shows the sale prices in dollars of each table and chair in three different years.

Based on the numbers and prices given in the tables, what is the highest possible sale price in dollars of a furniture set in 2007?

A) $320

B) $360

C) $400

D) $420

32

Age	Male	Female
0 - 18	4	5
19 - 35	7	6
36 - 65	14	3
66 - 90	4	1

The age of a random sample of people from a population is summarized in the table above. If the whole community consists of 31,000 people between the ages of 19 and 65, which of the following statements is true?

A) We expect that there are 15,200 females in the population.

B) We expect there are 5,580 females 65 years old and younger in the population.

C) We expect there are 9,300 females between 19 and 65 years old in the population.

D) We cannot determine the number of females in the population with the information given.

33

Average of 7 numbers is 68. Which number should be added to these numbers to increase arithmetic mean to 72?

A) 80

B) 90

C) 94

D) 100

34

$$n, 2n, 4n$$

The first term in the sequence above is n. If n is an integer and each term thereafter is equal to twice the previous term, which of the following could NOT be the sum of the first five terms of this sequence?

A) -62

B) 31

C) 124

D) 165

35

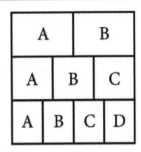

The square above is divided into 3 rows of equal areas. First row has two equal areas of A and B, second row has three equal areas of A,B and C, third row has four equal areas of A,B,C and D.

If a man fires a shot in succession, what is the probability that he will hit a region of B?

A) 0.333

B) 0.250

C) 0.361

D) 0.833

36

24-m, 24, 24+m

Which of the following is the arithmetic mean or average of the three quantities given above?

A) 8

B) 24

C) 8 + 2m/3

D) 8 + 3m

37

In a survey of a random sample of 1,500 residents aged 30 years or older from Essex County in New Jersey, 600 residents had a bachelor's degree or higher.

If the entire Essex county had 720,000 residents aged 30 years or older, around how many county residents would be expected to have a bachelor's degree or higher?

A) 288,000

B) 320,000

C) 360,000

D) 432,000

38

The arithmetic mean (average) of a and b is 12, and the average of c and d is 18. What is the average of a, b, c and d?

A) 3

B) 15

C) 30

D) 36

39

In a bag of 300 gummy bears, 20% of the gummy bears are blue, 70 of the gummy bears are red, 50 of the gummy bears are green in color, and the remaining are yellow.

What is the probability that the gummy bears picked will be yellow?

A) 0.20

B) 0.25

C) 0.30

D) 0.40

40

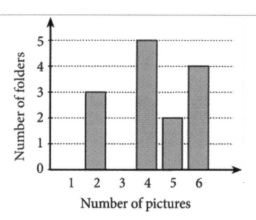

The number of pictures and folders is shown on the histogram given above.

Based on this histogram, which of the following is the arithmetic mean or average of pictures per folder?

A) 4

B) 4.29

C) 5.45

D) 6

41

Sport preference	Male	Female	Total
Basketball	8	2	10
Football	3	4	7
Baseball	7	3	10
Tennis	2	5	7
Ice hockey	5	1	6
Total	25	15	40

In Livingston High School a total of 40 high school students participate in sports. Based on the information given in the table above, what is the probability that a male student plays football?

A) 0.030

B) 0.050

C) 0.075

D) 0.120

42

$$\text{I.} \quad \frac{ma + nb}{2} \qquad\qquad \text{II.} \quad \frac{ma + nb}{m + n}$$

$$\text{III.} \quad \frac{ma + nb}{a + b} \qquad\qquad \text{IV.} \quad ma + nb$$

The average of m numbers is a and the average of n numbers is b. What is the average of all those numbers?

A) I

B) II

C) III

D) IV

43

Alice has taken 4 exams and her average score so far is 67. If she gets 100, a perfect score, on the remaining 2 exams, what will her new average be?

A) 62

B) 78

C) 89

D) 92

44

Machine A in casino Bellagio has three rotating wheels, called wheels K, L and M. Each wheel displays the following pictures: a banana, an orange, an apple, a candle and a dollar sign. The machine awards a cash prize to a player whenever wheels K and L land on either apple or orange and wheel M lands on a banana.

Assuming that for each wheel there is an equal probability of landing on each picture, what is the probability that the player will win a cash prize?

A) 0.008

B) 0.032

C) 0.064

D) 0.080

45

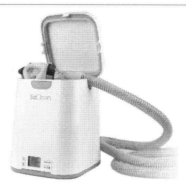

A Doctor wants to study the effectiveness of a CPAP Machine for sleep apnea. The Doctor records data on three groups of test subjects. The first group includes people who suffer from Apnea and are given the CPAP Machine. The second group includes people who suffer from apnea and are not given the CPAP Machine. The third group includes people who do not suffer from apnea and are given the experimental CPAP Machine.

Which of the following describes the research design for this study?

A) Observational study

B) Controlled experiment

C) Sample survey

D) None of the above

CONTINUE ▶

46

THESIS	
Parts in the thesis	6
Chapters in the thesis	14
Pages in the thesis	180
Number of words in the thesis	17,280

ALICE	
Number of hours Alice plans to write literature about her thesis each day	4
Number of words Alice writes per minute	12

Alice is planning to write her thesis. The tables above show the information about the thesis she aims to write and the amount of time she plans to spend writing the thesis each day.

If Alice writes at the rates given in the table, which of the following is the number of days it would take Alice to write the entire thesis?

A) 6

B) 10

C) 24

D) 96

47

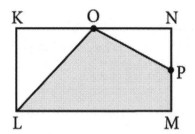

In rectangle KLMN above, O and P are the midpoints of sides KN and NM, respectively. What are the odds of a dart, thrown at random, landing in the shaded region?

A) 0.500

B) 0.625

C) 0.075

D) 0.080

48

If $a = b+c+d$, what is the average (arithmetic mean) of a,b,c,d in terms of a?

A) $\dfrac{a}{6}$

B) $\dfrac{a}{3}$

C) $\dfrac{a}{2}$

D) $2a$

49

A fashion model will wear any combination of five shirts, three belts and four skirts at Paris fashion show. How many different creations can be made from these apparels?

A) 12

B) 15

C) 30

D) 60

50

A boss decides to increase the salary of every one of his employees by \$500. How does the mean and median of the salaries change?

A) Mean and median does not change.

B) Mean increases by \$500, median stays same.

C) Median increases by \$500, mean stays same.

D) Both mean and median increases by \$500.

51

I. The median is higher than 60.

II. The mode is lower than 70.

III. The average score is above 60.

Seven students have taken a diagnostic test of mathematics and their scores, from lowest to highest, are as follows; 20, 30, 60, 60, 70, 80, 90.

Which of the statements given above are correct?

A) Only I

B) Only II

C) I and II

D) I, II and III

The arithmetic mean (average) of *a* and *b* is 8 and the average of *a,b* and *c* is 10. What is the value of *c*?

A) 4
B) 9
C) 14
D) 18

If the artithemetic mean(average) of the numbers M and N is P, what is the value of M in terms of N and P?

A) 2P - N
B) 2N - P
C) P - N
D) P - 2N

If a positive integer *m* is selected at random from the positive integers less than or equal to 10, what is the probability that $3m + 5$ will be less than and equal to 17?

A) 0.1
B) 0.2
C) 0.3
D) 0.4

There are two boxes. One box contains 6 red, 3 yellow balls, other box contains 2 blue, 3 green marbles. If one ball from each box is randomly drawn, what is the probability that a red and a blue ball will be drawn?

A) 0.27
B) 0.40
C) 0.67
D) 0.60

What is the nineth term of the arithmetic sequence whose first term is *n* and whose fourth term is $n+12m$?

A) $24m$
B) $32m$
C) $n+24m$
D) $n+32m$

17.0	17.5	18.0	18.0	19.0	19.0
19.5	20.0	20.5	20.5	21.0	26.0

Twelve values above are the measurements of length of a stick in inches. However 26.0 inches is an error. Which of the following changes most if the 26.0 inches measurement is removed?

A) Mode
B) Mean
C) Range
D) Median

58

The first term of a sequence is the number M. If each term thereafter is 3 greater than the term before, then what is the average (arithmetic mean) of the first eleven terms of this sequence?

A) M + 15

B) M + 165

C) 11M + 3

D) 11M + 165

59

DAYTIME TEMPERATURES IN CUPERTINO, CALIFORNIA						
Mon	Tue	Wed	Thu	Fri	Sat	Sun
67	79	76	70	79	78	71

Daytime temperatures, in degrees Fahrenheit, in Cupertino, California over a one-week period is given in the table above.

If F represents the most frequent temperature, A represents the arithmetic mean (average) of the temperatures and M represents the median temperature, which of the following is the correct order of F, A, and M?

A) A < F < M

B) A < M < F

C) M < A < F

D) M < F < A

60

A rental car company charges K dollars for the first week that a car is rented and L dollars for each day over one week.

What is the cost of renting a car for M days, where M is greater than 7?

A) K + L + M

B) K + L (M - 7)

C) K + 7 M

D) K + M (L - 7)

CONTINUE ▶

SECTION 4 - STATISTICS

#	Answer	Topic	Subtopic
1	C	TC	S4
2	C	TC	S8
3	B	TC	S8
4	D	TC	S4
5	B	TC	S8
6	C	TC	S8
7	D	TC	S8
8	D	TC	S8
9	C	TC	S8
10	B	TC	S4
11	C	TC	S4
12	A	TC	S4
13	D	TC	S8
14	D	TC	S4
15	D	TC	S4

#	Answer	Topic	Subtopic
16	C	TC	S4
17	C	TC	S8
18	C	TC	S8
19	D	TC	S4
20	C	TC	S8
21	A	TC	S4
22	D	TC	S4
23	B	TC	S4
24	B	TC	S8
25	C	TC	S8
26	A	TC	S8
27	C	TC	S4
28	B	TC	S4
29	D	TC	S4
30	B	TC	S8

#	Answer	Topic	Subtopic
31	C	TC	S4
32	C	TC	S8
33	D	TC	S8
34	D	TC	S8
35	C	TC	S4
36	B	TC	S8
37	A	TC	S8
38	B	TC	S8
39	D	TC	S4
40	B	TC	S8
41	D	TC	S4
42	B	TC	S8
43	B	TC	S8
44	B	TC	S4
45	B	TC	S8

#	Answer	Topic	Subtopic
46	A	TC	S4
47	B	TC	S4
48	C	TC	S8
49	D	TC	S4
50	D	TC	S8
51	B	TC	S8
52	C	TC	S8
53	A	TC	S8
54	D	TC	S4
55	A	TC	S4
56	D	TC	S8
57	C	TC	S8
58	A	TC	S8
59	B	TC	S8
60	B	TC	S8

Topics & Subtopics

Code	Description
SC4	Table Data & Probability
SC8	Statistics & Data Inferences

Code	Description
TC	Problem Solving and Data Analysis

165
CONTINUE ▶

1

Employees at a Bank				
Years Worked	Teller	Manager	Supervisor	Total
Less than 5	26	12	23	61
5 to 10	19	17	12	48
10 to 15	18	15	20	53
More than 15	17	11	10	38
Total	80	55	65	200

The table above shows the years worked by employees at a bank. What is the probability that a teller has worked for 5 or more years?

A) 27% $\frac{19+18+17}{80} = \frac{54}{80} = $ 67.5%

B) 32.5%

C) 67.5%

D) 80%

2

KLMNOPRKLMNOPRKLM...

1st   8th   15th

In the sequence of letters shown above, the first letter K is, followed by L, M, N, O, P and R.

Which of the following is the 41st letter in this sequence?

A) K   All of the following terms will be K

1st 8th 15th 22nd 29th 36th 43th

B) L

C) P

D) R

P R K
41th   43th

3

Sam has got the following grades on his tests; 78, 85, 98, and 82. He wants an 85 or better overall. What is the minimum grade Sam must get on the last test in order to achieve that average?

A) 72 $\frac{78+85+98+82+x}{5} \geq 85.5$

B) 82

C) 85 $343+x \geq 425$

D) 90 $-343 \qquad -343$

$x \geq 82$

4

A coin with two sides, heads, and tails, is flipped 4 times and the results are recorded. What is the probability that the 3rd flip results in tails?

A) 0.063   Every flip has a probability

B) 0.125   of $\frac{1}{2} = 0.5$

C) 0.250

D) 0.500

5

Mr. Avadis rasied all of his students' scores on a recent exam by 12 points. What effect did this increase have on the mean and median of the scores?

A) The mean and the median did not change.

B) The mean and the median increased by 12 points.

C) The mean increased by 12 points, but the median remained the same.

D) The median increased by 12 points, but the mean remained the same.

Both mean and median will increase because all scores are increasing.

6

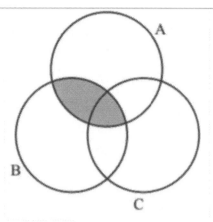

In the figure above, three circles represent single family houses on the Miami Beach. Circle A represents a house with an ocean view, Circle B represents a house with 5 bedrooms, and Circle C represents a house with a swimming pool.

What does the shaded region represent?

A) House with an ocean view, 5 bedrooms, and swimming pool

B) House with an ocean view and 5 bedrooms, but without swimming pool

C) House with an ocean view and 5 bedrooms (some possibly with swimming pool)

D) House with an ocean view and swimming pool (some possibly with 5 bedrooms)

Shaded region is mostly the intersection of A and B. Some of the area is also in C. So the answer is C.

7

$$m, 2m, n$$

If the artithemetic mean(average) of the 3 numbers given above is $2m$, then what is the value of n in terms of m?

A) $\dfrac{1}{2}m$ $\dfrac{m + 2m + n}{3} = 2m \cdot 3$

B) m $3m+n = 6m$ $n = \boxed{3m}$
           $-3m$ $-3m$

C) $\dfrac{3}{2}m$

D) $3m$

8

Sarah collected data on the weights of five newborn kittens. The weights of the kittens, in ounces, are; 12, 7, 6, 8, 12   Range = 12-6 = 6

6, 7, 8, 12, 12   Median = 8

Which statement regarding the mean, median, and range of the weights of the kittens is true?

Mean $= \dfrac{6+7+8+12+12}{5} = 9$

A) The mean is greater than the median, and the range is 12.

B) The median is greater than the mean, and the range is 12.

C) The median is greater than the mean, and the range is 7.

D) The mean is greater than the median, and the range is 6.

9

Lengths of Fish (in inches)						
9	7	10	11	8	10	11
11	12	12	12	12	13	13
14	14	15	15	15	16	25

7, 8, 9, 10, 10, 11, 11, 11, 12, 12, 12, 12, 13, 13, 14, 15, 15, 15, 16, 25

The lengths of a random sample of 21 fish are listed in the table given above, but the measurement of 25 inches is an error.

7, 8, 9, 10, 10, 11, 11, 11, 12, 12, 12, 12, 13, 13, 14, 15, 15, 15, 16

Which of the following would not be true when the 25-inch measurement is removed from the data?   Range before = 25-9 = 16

Range after = 16-9 = 7

A) Median does not change. Median is still 12

B) Mode does not change. Mode is still 12

C) Mean does not change. Mean will decrease

D) Range decreases. Range decreased from 16 to 7.

10

LINCOLN HIGH SCHOOL		
	Girls	Boys
Freshman	140	120
Sophomores	110	115
Juniors	112	124
Seniors	118	111

The chart above shows the grade level of girls and boys in Lincoln High School. If a boy is chosen at random, what is the probability that he is a junior?

A) 0.233   probability = $\dfrac{\text{desired outcomes}}{\text{all possible outcomes}}$

B) 0.264

C) 0.275 $= \dfrac{124}{120+115+124+111}$

D) 0.310

$= \dfrac{124}{470} = 0.264$

    168   CONTINUE ▶

11

How many different five-member teams can be made from a group of nine players, if each player has an equal chance of being selected?

Combination is a way to calculate the total outcomes where order of outcomes does not matter.

A) 36

B) 45

C) 126

D) 3,024

$$C(n,r) = \frac{n!}{(n-r)! \cdot r!} = \frac{9!}{(9-5)! \cdot 5!}$$

$$= \frac{9 \cdot 8 \cdot 7 \cdot 6 \cdot 5!}{4 \cdot 3 \cdot 2 \cdot 1 \cdot 5!} = 126$$

12

2, 4, 6, 8, 10, 12, 14, 16

If a number is chosen at random from the list given above, what is the probability that the number is divisible by 3?

A) 0.25

B) 0.33

C) 0.50

D) 0.75

Only 6 and 12 are divisible by 3.

$$\frac{desired}{all} = \frac{2}{8} = \frac{1}{4} = 0.25$$

13

Sales representatives realize that in Universal Studios for 100 tickets sold, toy shops sell 8 Transformer Robots at $35.00 each, 7 t-shirts of Shrek at $20.00 each, and 4 Harry Potter Illuminating Wand at $12.00 each. What is the arithmetic mean of these toy sales per ticket sold?

$$Mean = \frac{8 \cdot 35 + 7 \cdot 20 + 4 \cdot 12}{8 + 7 + 4}$$

A) $4.28

B) $4.68

C) $5.48

D) $24.63

$$= \frac{280 + 140 + 48}{19} = \frac{468}{19}$$

$$= 24.63$$

14

Given that there are 4 aces and 4 queens in a deck of 52 cards total, what is the probability of drawing neither an ace nor a queen from a deck of cards?

A) $\frac{2}{13}$

B) $\frac{4}{13}$

C) $\frac{8}{13}$

D) $\frac{11}{13}$

$$\frac{desired}{all} = \frac{52-8}{52} = \frac{44}{52} = \frac{11}{13}$$

CONTINUE ▶

15

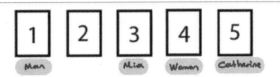

In the figure above, 5 parking lots are to be assigned to 5 employees; Ryan, Isabella, Mia, Giancarlo, and Cathrine. Ryan and Giancarlo are men and Isabella, Mia and Catherine are women.

The following conditions must be met:

• Parking lot 1 is assigned to a man.
• Catherine is assigned to Parking lot 5.
• Parking lot 4 is assigned to a woman.
• To each parking lot, a different employee must be assigned
• Mia is assigned to an odd-numbered parking lot and Ryan is assigned to an even-numbered Parking lot.

Which of the following employee is assigned to Parking lot 4?

A) Giancarlo
B) Ryan
C) Mia
D) Isabella

Mia can be assigned to 1, 3 or 5
1 is assigned to a man.
5 is assigned to Catherine
Then Mia will be assigned to 3
Because 4 will be assigned
to a woman, then Isabella will
be assigned to 4

16

If *m* is chosen at random from the set $\{4,5,7\}$ and *n* is chosen at random from the set $\{9,10,11\}$, what is the probability that the product of *m* and *n* is divisible by 5?

A) $\dfrac{1}{3}$

B) $\dfrac{4}{9}$

C) $\dfrac{5}{9}$

D) $\dfrac{2}{3}$

(4,9)   (4,10)   (4,11)
(5,9)   (5,10)   (5,11)
(7,9)   (7,10)   (7,11)

$$\frac{\text{desired}}{\text{all}} = \frac{5}{9}$$

Selections with 5 or 10 are divisible by 5.

17

Number of Students	Scores
3	90
9	80
7	70
4	65
6	55

Emily's score was accidentally omitted from the list given above. When her score is added, the arithmetic mean(average) of the class does not change. What is Emily's score?

If the average score does not change after adding Emily's score, then Emily's score is equal to the average score.

A) 67.9

B) 69

C) 71.4

D) 72

Average score $= \dfrac{3 \cdot 90 + 9 \cdot 80 + 7 \cdot 70 + 4 \cdot 65 + 6 \cdot 55}{3 + 9 + 7 + 4 + 6}$

Average score $= \dfrac{2,070}{29} = 71.4$

19

Amelia has 5 different skirts, 4 different pairs of pants, 6 different t-shirts, and 3 different jackets from which to choose when dressing for a party.

What is the total number of different combinations of 1 skirt, 1 t-shirt, 1 pair of pants, and 1 jacket?

A) 18

B) 30

C) 120

D) 360

$5 \cdot 4 \cdot 6 \cdot 3 = 360$

21

NUMBER OF EMPLOYEES		
Salary($)	Teacher	Manager
90,000 or more	30	10
Less than 90,000	90	40

The table above shows the number of employees in a school district which is classified according to personnel type and salary. If a teacher will be selected at random, what is the probability that the teacher's salary is over $90,000?

A) 0.25

B) 0.33

C) 0.50

D) 0.66

probability $= \dfrac{\text{desired outcomes}}{\text{all possible outcomes}}$

$\dfrac{30}{30+90} = \dfrac{30}{120} = \dfrac{1}{4} = 25\%$

22

Employees at a School				
Years worked	Nurse	Custodian	Teacher	Total
Less than 3	8	12	120	140
3 to 5	11	10	110	131
6 to 9	10	16	180	206
More than 9	12	14	120	146
Total	41	52	530	623

The table given above shows the years worked by employees at a school district. What is the probability of selecting a custodian who has worked for 6 or more years in the district?

A) 4.8%

B) 8.3%

C) 27%

D) 57.7%

Custodian worked more than 6 years

custodian

$\dfrac{16+14}{52} = \dfrac{30}{52} = 57.7\%$

23

A bag contains 7 red, 5 yellow, and 8 orange marbles. How many red marbles must be added into the bag so that the probability of randomly drawing a red marble is 0.48?

A) 3

B) 5

C) 12

D) 33

$$\frac{\text{Red marbles}}{\text{All marbles}} = \frac{7+x}{7+5+8+x} = \frac{48}{100}$$

$$\frac{7+x}{20+x} = \frac{12}{25}$$

After this step you can solve it for x or you can try options. x = 5 works.

$$25 \cdot (7+x) = 12 \cdot (20+x)$$

$$175 + 25x = 240 + 12x$$

$$\frac{13x}{13} = \frac{65}{13}$$

$$x = 5$$

24

The results of the survey conducted at Montville High School indicates that the median of the heights of all of the male students was 164 centimeters and the mode was 160 centimeters.

According to this information which of the following statements must be true?

A) There are no male students taller than 164 centimeters.

→ mode is the most frequent value

B) The most frequently occurring height of the male students is 160 centimeters.

C) The average (arithmetic mean) of the heights of the male students is 162 centimeters.

D) There are more male students who are 164 centimeters tall than those who are 160 centimeters tall.

25

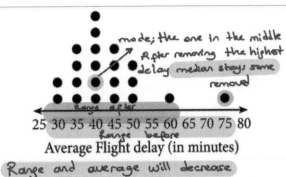

mode; the one in the middle
After removing the highest
delay median stays same
removed

Range after

Range before

Average Flight delay (in minutes)

Range and average will decrease

The average delay of flights for each of the largest 21 airline companies in Asia, was calculated and shown in the dot plot above.

If the highest flight delay is removed from the dot plot, which of the following changes occur?

A) The average will decrease only.

B) The average and median will decrease only.

C) The range and average will decrease only.

D) The median, range, and average will decrease.

26

Length of Cables
8 feet
10 feet
x feet
9 feet
7 feet
11 feet

A store has six different lengths of extension cables for sale. The length of the cables are shown in the table above. If the range of lengths of the six cables is 6 feet, what is the least possible value of *x*?

A) 5

B) 6

C) 16

D) 17

Range is the difference between the highest and lowest values.

Range = Highest − Lowest

6 = 11 − Lowest

Lowest = 5

27

Gender	Age Under 35	Age 35 or older	Total
Male	14	2	16
Female	5	4	9
Total	19	6	25

The table above shows the distribution of gender and age for 25 people who have taken a medical treatment in Saint Joseph medical center in Passaic County. If one person out of these 25 people will be selected at random, what is the probability that the selected will be either a female over age 35 or a male under age 35?

A) 0.28   female over 35 + male under 35
                     ─────────────────────────────
                                    25

B) 0.56

C) 0.72 $\frac{4+14}{25} = \frac{18\times4}{25\times4} = \frac{72}{100} = 0.72$

D) 0.76

28

If a fair dice is rolled twice, what is the probability that the first roll produces 3 and the second roll does NOT produce a 5?

A) 0.28   Probability of producing 3 is $\frac{1}{6}$

B) 0.139   Probability of NOT producing 5 is $\frac{5}{6}$

C) 0.166   To determine the probability of two independent events we multiply

D) 0.333   the probability of first event by the probability of the second event. So;

$$\frac{1}{6} \times \frac{5}{6} = \frac{5}{36} = 0.139$$

29

The candidates for a college are ranked by their high school GPA (Grade Point Average). There is an equal number of girls and boys in the application list, but more boys than girls are in the top 50% of the list.

Based on the information given above, which of the following statement must be true?

A) The highest ranked candidate is a boy.

B) The lowest ranked candidate is a girl.

C) There are at least 20 boys in the top 50% of the class.

D) There are more girls than boys in the bottom 50% of the class.

30

College Students' Sleep Habits		
Hours of Sleep	Uphill College	Frontier College
Average	5	7
Median	3	6
Mode	4	7
Standard Deviation	4	3

A random sample of students in two different colleges were surveyed for their sleep habits. The results are shown in the table below.

Which of the following statements is supported by the data given in this table?

A) More students attend Frontier College than Uphill College.

B) Variation of the hours of sleep per night among students at Uphill College is more than that of students' at Frontier College.

C) Less than half of the students at Uphill College get 6 hours of sleep per night.

D) More than half of the students at Uphill College get 5 hours of sleep per night.

Mode, median, and average are called the measures of central tendency. Standard deviation is a measure of variation. So we can only be sure about variation of hours of sleeping.

31

SCHOOL FURNITURE SETS			
Set	K	L	M
Desk	1	2	4
Chairs	6	5	2

PRICES			
Year	2002	2007	2012
Desk	$70	$80	$100
Chairs	$20	$40	$60

A school furniture company sells three sets of furnitures; set K, set L and set M. Each collection consists of a different number of tables and chairs as shown in the first table above. The second table given below the first one shows the sale prices in dollars of each table and chair in three different years.

Based on the numbers and prices given in the tables, what is the highest possible sale price in dollars of a furniture set in 2007?

A) $320   In 2007;

B) $360   set M: 4 × 80 + 2×40= 400

C) $400   set L : 2×80 + 5×40 = 360

D) $420   set K : 1×80 + 6×40 = 320

Because desks are more expensive for highest price you have to maximize number of desks.

32

Age	Male	Female
0 - 18	4	5
19 - 35	7	6
36 - 65	14	3
66 - 90	4	1

The age of a random sample of people from a population is summarized in the table above. If the whole community consists of 31,000 people between the ages of 19 and 65, which of the following statements is true?

$$19\text{-}65 \text{ years}: \frac{6+3}{6+3+7+14} = \frac{9}{30} \text{ female}$$

A) We expect that there are 15,200 females in the population.

B) We expect there are 5,580 females 65 years old and younger in the population. $\frac{9}{30} \times 31,000 = 9,300 \text{ female}$

C) We expect there are 9,300 females between 19 and 65 years old in the population.

D) We cannot determine the number of females in the population with the information given.

33

Average of 7 numbers is 68. Which number should be added to these numbers to increase arithmetic mean to 72?

A) 80 $7. \frac{\text{Sum of 7 numbers}}{7} = 68 \cdot 7$

B) 90 $\text{Sum of 7 numbers} = 476$

C) 94 $8. \frac{\text{Sum of 7 numbers} + x}{8} = 72 \cdot 8$

D) 100

$$\text{Sum of 7 numbers} + x = 576$$
$$476 + x = 576$$
$$-476 \qquad -476$$
$$x = 100$$

34

$$n, 2n, 4n$$

The first term in the sequence above is n. If n is an integer and each term thereafter is equal to twice the previous term, which of the following could NOT be the sum of the first five terms of this sequence?

A) -62

B) 31

C) 124

D) 165

Sum of the first five terms:

$n + 2n + 4n + 8n + 16n = 31n$

$n = -2 \qquad 31n = -62$

$n = 1 \qquad 31n = 31$

$n = 4 \qquad 31n = 124$

$31n$ can not be equal to 165

35

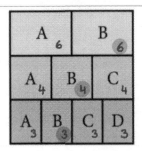

The square above is divided into 3 rows of equal areas. First row has two equal areas of A and B, second row has three equal areas of A,B and C, third row has four equal areas of A,B,C and D.

If a man fires a shot in succession, what is the probability that he will hit a region of B?

A) 0.333

B) 0.250

C) 0.361

D) 0.833

Three rows are divided into equal areas. If you assume each row has an area of 12 (LCM of 2,3, and 4) then;

$\dfrac{\text{Total area of } B}{\text{Total area}} = \dfrac{6+4+3}{36} = \dfrac{13}{36} = 0.361$

36

$$24-m, 24, 24+m$$

Which of the following is the arithmetic mean or average of the three quantities given above?

A) 8

B) 24

C) $8 + 2m/3$

D) $8 + 3m$

To find the average add up all the numbers and divide by how many numbers there are;

$\dfrac{24-m +24 +24+m}{3} = \dfrac{3\cdot24}{3}$

Average = 24

37

In a survey of a random sample of 1,500 residents aged 30 years or older from Essex County in New Jersey, 600 residents had a bachelor's degree or higher.

If the entire Essex county had 720,000 residents aged 30 years or older, around how many county residents would be expected to have a bachelor's degree or higher?

A) 288,000

B) 320,000

C) 360,000

D) 432,000

$\dfrac{600}{1,500} \times 720,000 = 288,000$

38

The arithmetic mean (average) of a and b is 12, and the average of c and d is 18. What is the average of a, b, c and d?

A) 3

B) 15

C) 30

D) 36

$\cancel{2} \cdot \dfrac{a+b}{\cancel{2}} = 12 \cdot 2 \qquad a+b=24$

$\cancel{2} \cdot \dfrac{c+d}{\cancel{2}} = 18 \cdot 2 \qquad c+d = 36$

$\dfrac{a+b+c+d}{4} = \dfrac{24+36}{4} = \dfrac{60}{4} = 15$

39

In a bag of 300 gummy bears, 20% of the gummy bears are blue, 70 of the gummy bears are red, 50 of the gummy bears are green in color, and the remaining are yellow.

What is the probability that the gummy bears picked will be yellow?

A) 0.20

B) 0.25

C) 0.30

D) 0.40

$300 \cdot \dfrac{20}{100} = 60$ Blue, 70 Red, 50 Green

$300 - (60+70+50) = 120$ Yellow

$\dfrac{\text{Number of yellow gummy bears}}{\text{Total number of gummy bears}} = \dfrac{120}{300} = 0.40$

40

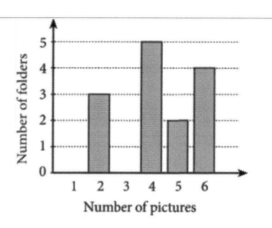

The number of pictures and folders is shown on the histogram given above.

Based on this histogram, which of the following is the arithmetic mean or average of pictures per folder?

A) 4

B) 4.29

C) 5.45

D) 6

$\dfrac{\text{Number of pictures}}{\text{Number of folders}} = \dfrac{2 \cdot 3 + 4 \cdot 5 + 3 \cdot 2 + 6 \cdot 4}{3 + 5 + 2 + 4}$

$= \dfrac{6 + 20 + 10 + 24}{14}$

$= \dfrac{60}{14} = 4.29$

41

Sport preference	Male	Female	Total
Basketball	8	2	10
Football	3	4	7
Baseball	7	3	10
Tennis	2	5	7
Ice hockey	5	1	6
Total	25	15	40

In Livingston High School a total of 40 high school students participate in sports. Based on the information given in the table above, what is the probability that a male student plays football?

A) 0.030

B) 0.050

C) 0.075

D) 0.120

# of male students playing football

# of male students

$$\frac{3 \times 4}{25 \times 4} = \frac{12}{100} = 0.12$$

42

I. $\dfrac{ma + nb}{2}$ II. $\dfrac{ma + nb}{m + n}$

III. $\dfrac{ma + nb}{a + b}$ IV. $ma + nb$

The average of m numbers is a and the average of n numbers is b. What is the average of all those numbers?

A) I

B) II

C) III

D) IV

$$\text{or.} \frac{\text{Sum of } m \text{ numbers}}{m} = a \cdot m$$

$$m \frac{\text{Sum of } n \text{ numbers}}{n} = b \cdot n$$

$$\frac{\text{Sum of } m \text{ numbers} + \text{Sum of } n \text{ numbers}}{m + n}$$

$$\frac{ma + nb}{m + n}$$

## 43

Alice has taken 4 exams and her average score so far is 67. If she gets 100, a perfect score, on the remaining 2 exams, what will her new average be?

A) 62

B) 78

C) 89

D) 92

$$\cancel{4} \cdot \frac{\text{Sum of the scores of 4 exam}}{\cancel{4}} = 67 \cdot 4$$

$$\text{Sum of the scores of 4 exam} = 268$$

$$\frac{268 + 200}{4 + 2} = \frac{468}{6} = 78$$

Machine A in casino Bellagio has three rotating wheels, called wheels K, L and M. Each wheel displays the following pictures: a banana, an orange, an apple, a candle and a dollar sign. The machine awards a cash prize to a player whenever wheels K and L land on either apple or orange and wheel M lands on a banana.

Assuming that for each wheel there is an equal probability of landing on each picture, what is the probability that the player will win a cash prize?

A) 0.008

B) 0.032

C) 0.064

D) 0.080

multiply the probabilities for K, L and M.

$$K \cdot L \cdot M$$

$$\frac{2}{5} \cdot \frac{2}{5} \cdot \frac{1}{5} = 0.032$$

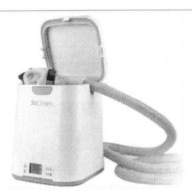

A Doctor wants to study the effectiveness of a CPAP Machine for sleep apnea. The Doctor records data on three groups of test subjects. The first group includes people who suffer from Apnea and are given the CPAP Machine. The second group includes people who suffer from apnea and are not given the CPAP Machine. The third group includes people who do not suffer from apnea and are given the experimental CPAP Machine.

Which of the following describes the research design for this study?

A) Observational study

B) Controlled experiment

C) Sample survey

D) None of the above

In controlled experiments all factors are kept constant except one.

THESIS	
Parts in the thesis	6
Chapters in the thesis	14
Pages in the thesis	180
Number of words in the thesis	17,280

ALICE	
Number of hours Alice plans to write literature about her thesis each day	4
Number of words Alice writes per minute	12

Alice is planning to write her thesis. The tables above show the information about the thesis she aims to write and the amount of time she plans to spend writing the thesis each day.

If Alice writes at the rates given in the table, which of the following is the number of days it would take Alice to write the entire thesis?

A) 6

B) 10

C) 24

D) 96

$4 \text{ hours} \times \frac{12 \text{ words}}{\text{minute}} = 4 \times 60 \text{ minutes} \times \frac{12 \text{ words}}{\text{minute}}$

$4 \text{ hours a day} ; 2,880 \frac{\text{words}}{\text{day}}$

$\frac{2,880 \text{ words}}{\text{day}} \times n \text{ day} = 17,280 \text{ words}$

$n = \frac{17,280}{2,880}$

$n = 6 \text{ days}$

47

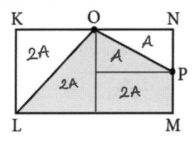

In rectangle KLMN above, O and P are the midpoints of sides KN and NM, respectively. What are the odds of a dart, thrown at random, landing in the shaded region?

A) 0.500

B) 0.625

C) 0.075

D) 0.080

$$\frac{\text{Shaded area}}{\text{Total area}} = \frac{5A}{8A} = 0.625$$

48

If $a = b + c + d$, what is the average (arithmetic mean) of a, b, c, d in terms of a?

A) $\dfrac{a}{6}$

B) $\dfrac{a}{3}$

C) $\dfrac{a}{2}$

D) $2a$

$$\text{Average} = \frac{a + b + c + d}{4} = \frac{a + a}{4} = \frac{a}{2}$$

49

A fashion model will wear any combination of five shirts, three belts and four skirts at Paris fashion show. How many different creations can be made from these apparels?

A) 12

B) 15

C) 30

D) 60

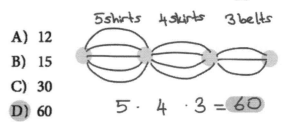

5shirts   4skirts   3belts

$5 \cdot 4 \cdot 3 = 60$

50

A boss decides to increase the salary of every one of his employees by $500. How does the mean and median of the salaries change?

A) Mean and median does not change.

B) Mean increases by $500, median stays same.

C) Median increases by $500, mean stays same.

D) Both mean and median increases by $500.   All the salaries are increasing.

51

~~I. The median is higher than 60.~~

Median is 60

✓ II. The mode is lower than 70.   *Mode is 60*

~~III. The average score is above 60.~~

20+30+60+60+70+80+90 = 410; $\frac{410}{7}$ = *58.57*

Seven students have taken a diagnostic test of mathematics and their scores, from lowest to highest, are as follows; 20, 30, 60, 60, 70, 80, 90.

Which of the statements given above are correct?

A) Only I

B) Only II

C) I and II

D) I, II and III

52

The arithmetic mean (average) of a and b is 8 and the average of a,b and c is 10. What is the value of c?

A) 4   *$1 \cdot \frac{a+b}{2} = 8 \cdot 2$*   *$a+b = 16$*

B) 9

C) 14   *$2 \cdot \frac{a+b+c}{3} = 10 \cdot 3$*   *$a+b+c = 30$*

D) 18   *$16 + c = 30$*

$-16 \quad -16$

$c = 14$

54

If a positive integer m is selected at random from the positive integers less than or equal to 10, what is the probability that $3m + 5$ will be less than and equal to 17?

A) 0.1   *$3m+5 \leq 17$*

       $-5 \qquad -5$

B) 0.2   *$\frac{3m}{3} \leq \frac{12}{3}$*

C) 0.3

D) 0.4   *$m \leq 4$*   *probability = $\frac{4}{10} = 0.4$*

55

There are two boxes. One box contains 6 red, 3 yellow balls, other box contains 2 blue, 3 green marbles. If one ball from each box is randomly drawn, what is the probability that a red and a blue ball will be drawn?

↳ means you will multiply the

A) 0.27   *probabilities of two independent event.*

B) 0.40

C) 0.67   *$\frac{6}{6+3} \cdot \frac{2}{2+3} = \frac{6}{9} \cdot \frac{2}{5} = \frac{12}{45} = 0.27$*

D) 0.60

56

What is the nineth term of the arithmetic sequence whose first term is n and whose fourth term is $n+12m$?

A) $24m$
B) $32m$
C) $n+24m$
D) $n+32m$

$a_n = a_0 + (n-1)\cdot d$
$a_4 = n + (4-1)\cdot d$
$n+12m = n + 3\cdot d$
$\frac{12m}{3} = \frac{3d}{3}$ $d = 4m$
$a_9 = n + (9-1)\cdot 4m$
$a_9 = n + 8\cdot 4m = n+32m$

57

$19.0+19.5/2 = 19.25$ median

| 17.0 | 17.5 | 18.0 | 18.0 | 19.0 | 19.0 |
| 19.5 | 20.0 | 20.5 | 20.5 | 21.0 | 26.0 |

17.0,17.5,18.0,18.0,19.0,19.0,19.5,20.0,20.5,20.5,21.0,26.0

Twelve values above are the measurements of length of a stick in inches. However 26.0 inches is an error. Which of the following changes most if the 26.0 inches measurement is removed? Median dropped to 19.0

17.0,17.5,18.0,18.0,19.0,19.0,19.5,20.0,20.5,20.5,21.0

A) Mode There is no mode, it does not change
B) Mean -26 over 12 numbers; decreases less than 5.
C) Range 26-17=9, 21-17=4; decreased by 5
D) Median 19.25-19.0 = 0.25, decreased by 0.25

58

The first term of a sequence is the number M. If each term thereafter is 3 greater than the term before, then what is the average (arithmetic mean) of the first eleven terms of this sequence?

1st 2nd 3^{d} .... 11th

A) $M + 15$
B) $M + 165$
C) $11M + 3$
D) $11M + 165$

$\frac{M + M+1\cdot3 + M+2\cdot3 +...+ M+10\cdot3}{11}$
$\frac{11M + 3\cdot(1+2+....+10)}{11}$
$11M + \frac{3\cdot(\frac{1+10}{2})\cdot10}{11}$
$\frac{11M+165}{11} = M+15$

59

DAYTIME TEMPERATURES IN CUPERTINO, CALIFORNIA						
Mon	Tue	Wed	Thu	Fri	Sat	Sun
67	79	76	70	79	78	71

Daytime temperatures, in degrees Fahrenheit, in Cupertino, California over a one-week period is given in the table above.

If F represents the most frequent temperature, A represents the arithmetic mean (average) of the temperatures and M represents the median temperature, which of the following is the correct order of F, A, and M?

A) $A < F < M$ 79 is the most frequent one
B) $A < M < F$ 67 70 71 76 78 79 79
C) $M < A < F$ A < M < F
D) $M < F < A$ Average will be less than 76 because number on the left deviate more from the median.

A rental car company charges K dollars for the first week that a car is rented and L dollars for each day over one week.

What is the cost of renting a car for M days, where M is greater than 7?

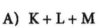
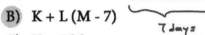

A) K + L + M

B) K + L (M - 7)

C) K + 7 M

D) K + M (L - 7)

Made in the USA
Middletown, DE
17 June 2022

67288374R10113